£10

CW01108874

LOOSE

A LOST AND FOUND TIMES ANTHOLOGY

WATCH

INVISIBLE BOOKS

LOST AND FOUND TIMES

was a conceptual stunt dreamed up by myself and the painter Doug Landies in 1975: a sheet of fake lost and found notices to be slipped under the windshield wipers of cars in the parkinglot of Graceland Shopping Center, near where I live. Since we were both doing mail art, naturally many copies went out in the mail, and many correspondents replied by sending in their own notices. Thus a second issue was born. We decided we wanted a book for the third issue, so we expanded into using literary and graphic work as well as the lost and found notices. The fourth issue was a collaboration between Landies and myself (his drawings and calligraphy, my poems). Then, in 1978, Landies suddenly died; simply fell over dead due to an undiagnosed heart condition. I was shocked and dismayed, and put together a fifth issue of LAFT dedicated to the work of my friend and collaborator.

I continued the magazine, having found that I enjoyed reading and publishing unusual work, work that at the time no one else seemed to be publishing, and LAFT very quickly took on the basic format it has today. Obviously the kind of work has changed somewhat as the times and my tastes have changed. Its readership and number of contributors have expanded considerably as well, and there are a surprising number of truly illuminated institutions and individuals who have been careful to acquire a complete collection. (Which can still be purchased, by the way, though maybe not for long, so you'd better act fast.)

LOS

FOU
TIM

This anthology aims at presenting a representative sampling of what LAFT has meant over the years. It is not comprehensive in any way, and far too many brilliant works and personalities are missing. But it gives an excellent sense of the flavor of the magazine, where it has been, as well as many of its most brilliant pages.

This selection also, of course, suggests an eccentric and stimulating aesthetic, one which continues to evolve, and which I will leave to the reader to characterize, if he or she is inclined to theorize. The process of editing LAFT has been an important ingredient in the development of my own style as a poet, because in being forced to choose the few pieces among the thousands that come to my mailbox, I am clarifying and developing my own conception of what's interesting and good. Thus LAFT is, for me, a vital part of the context in which my own work takes form. My hope is that its regular gatherings will form such a context for its other readers and contributors as well. I am grateful to Invisible Books for making the strange and dynamic culture of LAFT more visible to all.

John M. Bennett

May 1998

O
USE
WAT
CH

Lost and Found Times

ADVERTISE FREE!

SEND YOUR NOTICES TO EITHER EDITORIAL OFFICE!

No. 1, August 1975

Offices:

Luna Bisonte Prods
137 Leland Ave.
Columbus, Ohio 43214

Studio Mr. Sensitive
118 E. Longview Ave.
Columbus, Ohio 43202

LOST: Cigarbox of twisted doubleedged razor blades. Important life's work. Generous reward. 934-2236.

FOUND: Zenith color TV Hi-Fi consol. Found in drainage ditch, Circleville Rd. 946-3509.

LOST: Rubber doll head, r. eye crushed. Sentimental value. Reward. 724-8670 after 3.

LOST: Goldlook snake ring with rubylook eyes. Call 268-0681 eves. Ask for Nick. Big reward.

STOLEN: Orange plastic ERA bottle, crack in bottom, pink bow around cap. Wife heartbroken. 445-2387 all day.

FOUND: Rubber gorilla embracing rear window dancing grass skirted vinyl HOOLAH LADY. Bound with red cord. Come pick it up at Nettles Exxon.

FOUND: Unmarked carton filled with catheads. Claim immediately! 999-3267.

LOST: Large silver painted plaster skull with back of head bashed in. Reward - sentimental value. 439-4421.

LOST: Case of sealed canning jars containing pieces of paper with brown smears on them. Must be kept cold! Contact Fred at Mort's Meat Lockers, 427-3892.

LOST: At Festival of the Lights one hand made inverted gag-chicken pendant. Call Dottie at the Chicken Shack, nights.

FOUND: Photo album with family snapshots, left eye cut out of each person photographed. Vicinity Southern Hotel. 984-7321 before 10.

LOST: My yodelling parakeet, in the vicinity of Lacluster Apts. Needs beak medication desperately. Yellow green. Call 846-4126, home all day. I miss that little yodel.

LOST: Red velvet flocked tail-pipe extension, glass eyes glued around flared tip, vicinity Graceland. Child in tears. Stew's Texaco, 263-5587.

LOST: While getting off the boat, one pair of custom made image inversion spectacles. Willem, N.Y.C. 212-337-6841.

LOST: Copy of "Motel Sex Club" by Bub Whiel with every sentence underlined. Reward! 888-8742.

FOUND: A bag containing bull worker muscle tone kit, assorted ping pong assesories, 3 sealed jars of unknown larva, a bundle of love letters addressed to Occupant, and a two-flap day-glo orange hunting cap (size 8 1/2). Found Sunday. St. Alonzo chapel. Ask for Nick. 268-0682.

LOST: Plastic "Goldlife" ID bracelet with chain, engraved DIRTSUCK. Great sent. value, reward. Pete at Rod's Plumbing and Blacktop Coat, 846-4262, evenings.

LOST: I lost my prized goat bladder dress gloves at the Spring Nurses' Dance. If you took them by mistake please return them. No questions asked. 321-1703.

LOST: Leather case containing ladies spikeheeled and needletoed shoes, painted black and coated with grease. High reward. Call Jojo at 845-8469 after 4 AM.

FOUND: Woven wire bird proof lime alloy acoustically adjusted self-annealling novelty cellulose boutique cabana shirt with beeswax charm buttons. Ask for the mgr. at Carlo's Banana Boat Club.

FOUND: Man's wallet with coin-op photobooth pictures of broken children's toys. Call Jonnie at the Rod Shop.

FOUND: Chair upholstered with pink shag carpeting, skull embroidered on backrest. Culvert county 14 near Phartersberg. Dan's Gulf and Worms.

LOST: Personal diary, "I am Spitman, slick and together" written cover. Please don't read! Call Slim at 437-9447 anytime day or night.

THE DEATH OF JIM JORDAN

Oh Jimmy, all sweetness has gone out of us. All light sleeps. All pretty trees weep. Jimmy J is dead and no one knows the answer. No one knows what to say. It was a snowy night. It was so cold and so white and Jimmy couldn't see, white white white all over, the highway like a funnel of darkness, a frightened deer bolted in front of the car, Jimmy (always a lover of animals) swerved the car and skidded uncontrollably over a steep embankment into a frozen river. He was killed instantly.

YOU CANT DO THAT.

YOU CANT DO THAT.

It was a small ceremony. B Schwartz, stunned, but looking stunning in an antique black mourning veil, black gloves, a black chemise, black pillbox hat, black shoes, flew in from San Francisco, stood vacantly, alien to family and local friends, isolated in the ice of grief, the blank, desolate island of desolation, unable to cry or think, unable to move, stood by the grave as the other mourners walked solemnly away, and as Mrs. Jordan passed, gently, almost unnoticed, touched her sleeve (black crepe), and she glanced, nearly imperceptibly, their eyes met, felt the sudden recognition. . . . "We are one." Then left with the others, as B stood, frozen. Is death the only mystery left. The one reality, hard clear and final, the only pure truth. B is able to think only in images, which are shining under the plexiglass of time. Is memory all that is left . . . does nothing move beyond—what. She drops the single black rose to the grave and walks away.

JIMMY J, JIMMY J.

There was a telephone call, that terrifying icey ring at three in the morning mother runs to the phone in her nightgown, the pause on the other end of the line. . . .

YOU CANT DO THAT.

Jimmy J is gone, there is little that can happen, the memory is an unbearable tenderness.

Nothing is said. The voice is caught. The hand gestures in empty air, rests at the collar, twists a mother-of-pearl button, falls to the side. No one speaks. The light is somehow changed. With him, all sweetness passes. Nothing is the same.

Rene White

Ray Johnson

Most sincerely yours,
JATAKA
RAY JOHNSONG
TOILET PAPER
LOST: Bed pan.
SPAM BELT CLUB
DEAD PAN CLUB
BLUE EYES CLUB
BRUE EYES CRUB

Douglas C. Landies

From the desk of

LUCKIE MUDFLAPP

dear NIK-

I know what you mean about self-centered- when I try to find the center of me self so hard I gets self centered,

Al Agua

nips in day

She slams the phone the paper
smeared across her desk she gasps and
stares real hard at the cardboard doggies
taped upon her window
Nick he turns away from this, gives his
three-tiered rubber stamping rack a whirl
and heads off toward the computer terminals

Something quivers in the lightsheets above
his head his face fades out in the blackscreen mirror,
numbers popsnap over it his eyes a nine
that pulses crakks away You're only here to
scream and pound on babies,
drive your way to stacks of receipts left in
the trash on Thursdays, It's like that Mr. Coffman,
fixes your furnace, says the gasco rips him off, the
only thing he loves is his grandchild, bright and
gasping, heading for the payroll office and his
40 daily hours that pile like rocks
in his acid corndog sack, Thank God, he says,
I need that wrap, that fleshy core, that
guts I toss and choff on a wooden stick

He hears a groan come out his body he moves
home speeding in his chestskin, I see it, Dreameat
Beauty Salon, pinkish mirrors that wheel around some
numbers Back At One he thinks he sits in the tub
the lights were in and out he saw some
bright red monkeys with eyes were pink and black
downstairs he heard the dogs beneath the kitchen clock,
eating diapers, chewing at the floor

After Just One Tube he says I may look 35 but
actually I'm 65 and Zero Makeup Has Been Used he
ends his day he chews his dayglo pottie toidie brutsch
he sees his wife a stick of smoking time between her lips
From The Bottom Of The Bottle Ms Splits he
sings and decorates her tits with friction tape

John M. Bennett

Douglas C. Landies

DOG CAKE HAT

The dog had on a wedding cake it was
barking at a buglight hanging off the wall
Nips was staring at the tabletop
thought the greasespots eyes
Looks like yer maw served up he
said his shirt tightening on his back
Yer hat's on fire! she screams
and covers his head with the garbage bucket

Later he dreamed a toaster, electric green
smoke towering out of it, he was
walking behind the shopping center
saw a word fall off the roof, DOGHAT it said
crashing on the empty bins

In the basement he filled a box with cockroach poison
thought his hair was growing stiff and
saw a light spiraling on the furnace;
he grabbed his tools, fell on the stairs
I'll have to change my plans he thought
the hammer speeding toward his face

John M. Bennett

apr 20

I was staying at Columbus Ohio I recall not where & check the big map on the wall like the kind in the Boston subway terminals to look for Leland Ave & find it in the streetlist so I take a ride on my bicycle over to 137 Leland Ave to visit John M Bennett while in town. Its quite a ways off but I am there in a jiffy & park my bike by the giant house overlooking a dusty shrubbed ravine down in which two men are setting up an eight-paneled folding display (you know the hinged type with wooden legs) which shows various 12″ x 12″ indeterminate visuals by John M Bennett. By time I get down there to take a few photos (had my camera) theyve moved it to another location. They keep setting it up & moving it again. One man was I believe somewhat short w/curly black hair. The other taller & long straight blond hair wire-rim glasses a moustache maybe a beard. I ask him are you John M Bennett. He guardedly mumbles yes & I introduce myself my name is Steve Hitchcock. He doesnt acknowledge recognition but starts talking in some quietly jabbering language & giggling as I follow him & his friend in the swinging plateglass doors of the house. I respond fluently without knowledge of what I am saying & John M Bennett laughs. I am left alone in the kitchen or somewhere & I end up wandering from room to room alone or sometimes among people I dont know but I end up repeatedly going back to the previous room to get the flash unit I had left idly behind with some black strips of paper. Eventually I find a cubbyhole emitting a shuffling woodenly mechanical noise & cans of household cleaner spray paint & the like in the corner. I see a square opening in the floor to another room. Down there I can see a top shelf w/books their titles on the spine facing up. The noise is from some sort of funhouse double-ladder. Between the ladders the rungs are covered with full-size bed-pillows so when you descend between alternating shuffling up-&-down ladders you are rubbed mysteriously. The space between is so small I can only get my leg in to my knee so I climb down the sides. I find myself in the darkened bedroom of John M Bennett surrounded by young smiling girls in bedclothes in their teens it appears. Their faces are all powdered grey & pallid & their eyes blackened. Each one looks like a model of Linda Blair in her demonic transition. They all grin hideously smacking their lips & some fiddling w/themselves through their dirty nighties. John M Bennett is lying over beyond his bed in this small room in a green robe of the material of which sweatshirts are made as one of these little demon babes is stroking his forehead. I climb back out w/the feeling that at any moment all these girls will pounce at me & tear my mortal flesh to ribbons. Later on the living room couch John M Bennett removes his shirt & drops his pants to show me something I hope I never see again (out of the ghoulish mind of HP Lovecraft). His body becomes leathery & hirsute. Goatlike & brown-haired. His sex organ is blackened half-penis & barbed scrotum w/hermaphroditic repulsive hugemouth vulva & white cunt teeth. He is lying on his back on the couch I stand behind & stroking the empurpled lips w/two dwarfed pair of hind legs scaled & hooved (hooves are cleft) while fucking himself w/two clawed appendages that wriggle out from his crotch. With one front paw all scaly & dog-clawed he strokes my hand. I think to myself no wonder this guy is so freaky.

Steve Hitchcock

(c) Eva de Jolsvay & John M. Bennett 1979 Luna Bisonte Prods

POEM COVERED WITH MOSS

The expenditure of effort.
The scarification.
The efficient renunciations.
The class action suit.
The pause.
The freedom sting.
The lapel of yours. The ground.
The medical school.
The coat of liquor.
The razor blade and the ham.
The ratiocinations.
The end product.
The chuckling house. The air
foil twins giving lead time
to the corpuscle.
The Jones.
The lust.
The voice breaking over noodles.
The stashed quip boil
taken at school.
The clemencies.
The incarcerated dice and their
factory decal nap slaughtered with a lute.
The color separations.
The dervish awl put in a gun.
The hot plot.
The cork.
The blue. The shawm.
The hologram permanently fused
to a circus-breakfast white.
The bonkers.
The turkey blues.
The land of gallant rope.
The cuckold.
The story of a palace trout.
Ah, the story of a palace trout.

Peter Frank

C. Mehrl Bennett

ITS MONKEYMEAT MAKES ME THIS COLOR

slow as a virus of tires, sacred mantra in the stop
light, those 17 syllables granny mumbled over & over
committing suicide kapusta, the fish in suit & tie
obviously a relative;
of elephant congestion, needed repair, wax
orbit opportunities, coined coal,
long saffron robes without clingfree,
sawdust in the bread, tie in the toothpaste,
baby ate his ibm selectric, ratchet v's in evinrude, trees
ablaze w/ snails, mainmast denim boredom stars, stump
or multidigital sheep lightning, open cans of salmoneyes
deerflux, lace reaped seas, the sugar demands footchip the,
zits for a hero,
toadhats, cube of hemlock
seeking rewards, open as buckeyes,
coupons of revolution

Dan Raphael

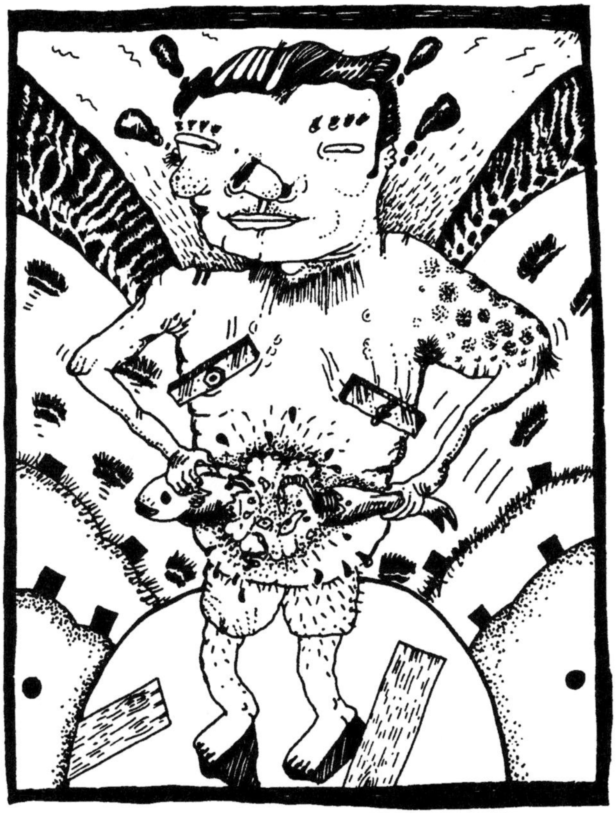

Her eyesight fluid as she
turned the map to automatic
and raised the lid of the mirror box
the veins in the palm of her foot
were throbbing as she caressed the wall
"Windows are not creatures" she
said and laid her face upon the table

John M. Bennett & C. Mehrl

THE SENSE OF UNWASHED SHANKS AS PROUST'S CAKE

In long-handles I think I might resemble him,
Sweetheart. Streak my hair yellow as well as gray
And claw my beard fully to whiskers, then I
Could say *Uncle George!* surprizing myself
In the bathroom mirror, just as the odd thought
Of him, after it must be twenty years or
More, surprized me last night, caught me unawares.
Well it filled me with glee. Bull joy. Enter
The crammed pigeonholes of Time's musty desk
Is a small death compared to real felark
Of Uncle George's rooms. Hairs, long brown ones,
As from a closet brush, Oz lion's bad cough,
Were braided up his sofa-arms in tufts,
Drying like drowned horses' manes. But not quite dry.
Sweetheart, a pound of okra filled his seat,
I swear it. When, therefore, my great-aunt's
Whiskper, beating away the mottled air
Like a countrywoman's broom, failing
At that, as the fainted July sun flicking
And flicking itself against the sticky green
Black candy windows of George's shack,
Said *Why he hasn't had a bath since Mame died,*
Was unavailed, because he was deaf, and
He *was* unwashed, I felt, sweetheart, such love
For that old unwashed man, it near to tore
My head off, and shit in my neck. Saint George.
We sense sanctity how late. Your remark
Brought it back to me last night. When you said
You need a bath. When you said I smell your taint.

Al Ackerman

I had a dream the sirens woke me at 7 am a black squall line to the west the billboard at 9 & Grosebeck was showing commercials like films instead of a flat advert then I got my mail a cassette from Richard H Kirk & from Nips and Lady C was 4 boxes of cake mix & some mirro-writing rubberstamp work of Nips with death images then next day for real got a card from Nips with a axe in meat head.

Michael Dec

BURNED SOFA STORY

many years ago brooklyn joe jones, artist extraordinary, visited al hansen and stayed at his loft in east broadway in new york city. he drank a few beers too many, dozed off with a lighted cigarette, and set the loft afire. the destruction was distressing, if not total.

some years later brooklyn joe jones, artist extraordinary, visited me in vermont. he drank a few beers too many, dozed off with a lighted cigarette, and set my big couch afire. the destruction was distressing, if not total.

he now lives in asolo in italy.

nyc 14.iii.80

Dick Higgins

ONETABLEONETABLE

15:4:81
15 AUG 1980

She saw a burned black sofa on shimmering black dots.

Robin Crozier

MOST OF MY DAYS WERE SPENT IN FIXING PEOPLE WHO HAD ALREADY SPENT CONSIDERABLE TIME FIXING ME

A&A	He aroused me: I abducted him
	He abhored me: I abandoned him
B&B	He buffeted me: I broke him
	He bucked me: I buried him
C&C	He cajoled me: I condemned him
	He chastised me: I cheated him
D&D	He depreciated me: I debauched him
	He deceived me: I destroyed him
E&E	He extricated me: I extradited him
	He exhorted me: I expelled him
F&F	He frustrated me: I flayed him
	He feted me: I fought him
G&G	He graded me: I granulated him
	He greeted me: I gored him
H&H	He heckled me: I hurt him
	He humiliated me: I hackled him
I&I	He ignored me: I identified him
	He idolized me: I impeached him
J&J	He jangled me: I jailed him
	He jeered me: I juggled him
K&K	He kidnaped me: I knifed him
	He knocked me: I knighted him
L&L	He lashed me: I larruped him
	He liberated me: I lacerated him
M&M	He maddened me: I macadamized him
	He maligned me: I mangled him
N&N	He nauseated me: I nominated him
	He nudged me: I nullified him
O&O	He ogled me: I ossified him
	He oppressed me: I ostracized him
P&P	He pacified me: I penalized him
	He pampered me: I parboiled him
Q&Q	He quoted me: I quelled him
	He qualified me: I quailed him
R&R	He rankled me: I radicated him
	He rehabilitated me: I resigned him
S&S	He scolded me: I slew him
	He soothed me: I starved him
T&T	He tired me: I trampled him
	He tolerated me: I tyrannized him
U&U	He urged me: I undermined him
	He underwrote me: I unnerved him
V&V	He venerated me: I vilified him
	He vexed me: I violated him
W&W	He worried me: I whipped him
	He wrenched me: I wounded him
X&X	He xed me: I x-rayed him
	He xipped me: I xystered him
Y&Y	He yanked me: I yowled him
	He yoked me: I yapped him
Z&Z	He zed me: I zanied him
	He zested me: I zeroed him

Bern Porter

THE TANKAS

Collander hatched stones
with sufficient breathing space
to sing moon moon sing
to the pickle of Kaph at
whose tip an eye opens wide

To wear india
ink instead of socks and hop
instead of warming
formula against the hand
puppets spattering concrete

Menageries float
face up on the word for sea
and amount to domes
between salt-flushed night risings
stewed in gold and refashioned

Right across your face
why did you steal my watch? hums
the lattice formal
as a drum baked in the leaves
with earth's slow passion tuning

The comb is honeyed
from your hair at places where
the train has breath prints
on its metal skin that lasts
the ventures without feeling

Cement mixer churns
ironic sequel to the
rainbow wings thrashing
through long black grass where
toadstools
look through like noses and bark

Burphy Slacks, Jr.

A SMALL FLASH GOES OFF

In Los Angeles I go to a movie theatre to watch an Alfred Hitchcock film. Who should greet me when I walk in, but Alfred Hitchcock, sitting in a director's folding chair. After the show, I walk down a street lined with old, shuttered houses. JoAnn is with me. I want to find out if any of the houses are for rent, but there isn't anyone around to ask. Then we run into John Bennett, who says he lives nearby. He gives us his phone number, smiles nervously and goes on his way.

JoAnn runs up to a liquor store and feet first, jumps through the plate glass window on which is painted a Budweiser logo "Pick a Pair of Sixpacks." The window shatters, throwing glass all over the sidewalk. She lands inside. Seconds later, JoAnn leaps back through the window with two sixpacks. Then she does what I fear most. She walks into a bank, hands a teller a note demanding money and, pointing to me outside, tells the guard not to move. The teller quickly fills her arms with bundles of crisp banknotes. After tearing the phone out of the wall, JoAnn walks outside and together we run like hell to a shopping center parking lot. While walking behind a long row of parked cars, a man runs up to us. I tell JoAnn to cover the money with my shirt, which I quickly remove and hand to her. We keep walking toward the sidewalk. I try to get rid of the man, who tells me he knows me and that his wife is going to have a baby. He says this worries him a lot. I tell him of all the bad things that will happen to him – he'll go crazy, become an alcoholic, go broke, and his cock will fall off. He leaves in tears.

From the shopping center we walk to a residential neighborhood. The sidewalks are lined with the tallest banana trees I have ever seen. They form a canopy, cool and luxurious, under which we feel safe. After a while, we exit onto a busy intersection. I go to a phone booth and call John Bennett, who says come over – but he can't come get us, so we take a taxi. When we arrive at his house, John is pleased but suspicious. JoAnn and I go into a bedroom and hide the money. Suddenly, I hear voices outside and then a loud knocking on the front door. John, not knowing what, lets the people in. I look through a window and see a police bus parked in front of the house. Then I imagine myself as a Genet sort of character and realize I will spend years in prison where I will go mad and write. JoAnn and I are not upset – the chase was fun. Then a small flash goes off and I wake up, feel reckless and rich.

Francis Poole

1. the tip of a rubber glove
2. one burnt potato
3. one black heart

go to the safeway store. buy a beef heart. put it in the toaster
oven and turn it on broil 500. forget about it. in two hours the
phone rings. it is the one you think you love. you are enveloped
in the stench of a burning black heart that you have not noticed
because you forgot, but stepping back to answer the phone, who is the
person you think you love, you notice. oh, something is burning, hold
please. take the heart and put it in a jar with a label on it.
go back to the phone and continue.
take four steps, there is blood on my pants,
take four steps and start the dance.
stilted stick movements, jerky and smart,
he has an ass like a strawberry tart.

i think i want to die.
empty blacked heart, someone forgot to take it out of the oven.
take four steps and do a jig,
then four more and take a swig.
cry tomorrow, then yesterday,
go for a roll in some yellow hay.
i think i want to die, or
have my insides scraped, red and black laid out on a table,
a new map, some new territory, a long red vein is a road to Illinois,
a small town, a clot on the floor, a piece of intestine is a wide field,
a strand of hair, a cow.

(every minute that is spent with the insides of a burnt cow's heart here,
in the chest instead of my own red fist, every second, every pulse beat
with this blackened mass inside, there like that, every minute spent
like this eats away at my tenderness.
this is what cancer must be like.)

Sabina Ott

It ing es our on not
go in he owl The he went she es
us at at on us an are
bi ges are at am do cow
in hening out our has gois
Is is initing can flies come and
we cut was bus owl dored
doll cat car blue from on
es nest her cut it barning
pastetous we has go green
bus us to mine did be by to see
saw his her have live get for
to too n cut cow am ride at
on make not can can chickens.

Scott Helmes

A STORY

As I sat in the tiny smoke-filled bathroom, sweat glinting in the tile grout beside a mistorn sheet of perforated tissue, *I felt the throbbing of my missing eye.* Hub-bub, Torque, Snotty – yesterday's words ricocheted off the cracked porcelain. *"If only she hadn't ripped off my shirt", I thought.* A small bubble of gas lifted into my larnyx. *"If only I hadn't spit in her purse".*

Mellon Park B, the 11:15 crosstown, had jumped a curb and pinched *a tiny man against the trunk of a red Datsun. His squeals* of delight sounded a treble accompaniment with a pounding *in the roots of my eyes. I clutched my* moist pencil stub and pressed its dark blunt tip.

John M. Bennett & Davi Det Hompson

MYSTERY STORY

There was a crown lying on the concrete floor
where it had just rolled away from the dead man's fingertips,
but he wasn't a king.
Was he an actor? the detective asked.
No.
Was he ambitious?
Yes.

Why was he lying on his back on the red floor looking up, his face
turning away empty, looking at nothing, his eyes
rolled up, his shoulders in a shrug?
Why was there no blood at all in the body?
Why hadn't he cleaned the chocolate stain on his tie?
Was he careless about his blood, or his ties?
No.
Did he know, then, that he was about to die?
Yes.

If robbery was the motive, why were a hundred dollars
fanned out carefully in a circle around the body?
If revenge was the motive, whom had he wronged?
No one.
If fear or hatred or pleasure was the motive, who might have killed him?
Anyone.

The detective examined the room. Locked doors, no windows,
no way in or out, no footprints, even his own, in the blood,
no motives, means or opportunity, no suspects, no confessions likely.
There were problems here, all right, but he would solve them.
He always did. But first he would have to learn
what the white face on the floor already knew:
nothing is secret until the wrong questions
hide all the answers; but about the acts
that draw a man from nothing into life, or bludgeon him back to death,
there is only one right question, asked by those who know
nothing, understand nothing, assume nothing.

The detective lay down beside the dead man.

Edward Lense

ETERNAL CULTURE DiSCOVERED

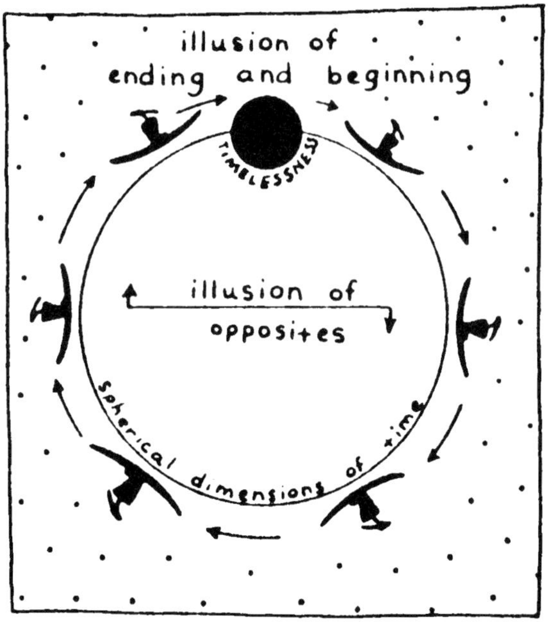

The explorer known as Madam X has brought news of a timeless culture which she encountered during her journey through the eternal segment of the time sphere.

According to eternal culture all time and dimension moves in one overall direction around the sphere, creating an illusion of opposites as well as an illusion of beginning and ending.

Beings of the eternal culture, understanding the design of the time sphere, see the eternal history of time and dimension as a unity, encompassing the opposites in dimension and the variations in time.

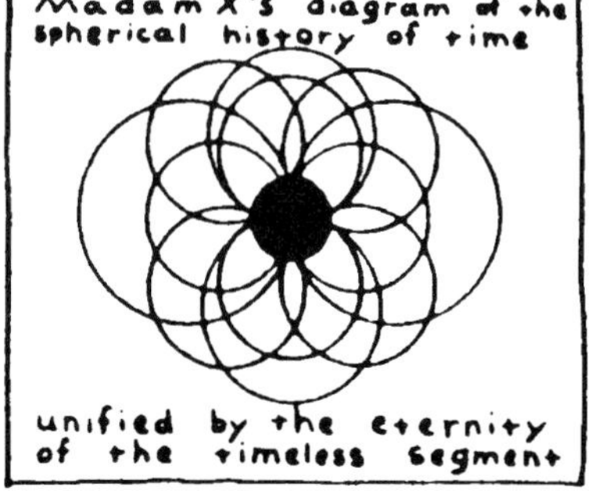

Madam X's diagram of the spherical history of time
unified by the eternity of the timeless segment

According to Madam X this spherical view of the infinite variety of phenomena has enabled the eternal culture to expand consistantly, without internal friction, and so move far ahead into the future.

EDiTORiAL

The circumnavigation and proof of the spherosity of time alters our point of view.

ADVERTISEMENT

NEW
OLD
Madam X
BRAND
FULLY
GUARANTEED
FOREVER
SPHERiCAL
TiMELESS

SEQUENCING: THE PARKWAY AT 4 a.m.

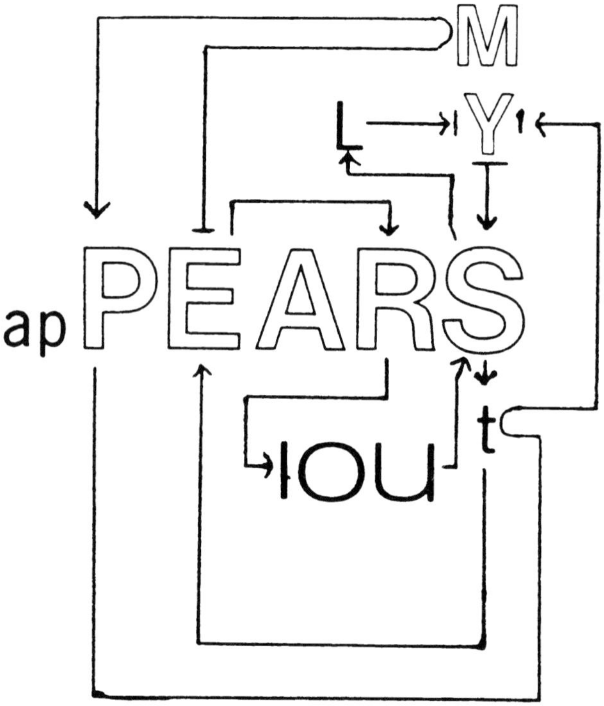

K.S. Ernst

TO MY FRIEND
("in the manner of the poems of Leopardi")

You would abandon me? An out-of-towner
fellow poet—just today I've lost my shirt
all my books and papers torn
like an amnesty note to enemies
who invite me over then slam the door!
Bastard, I'm no Witness hustling *Watchtower*,
but on Saturday morning I can spot a con
when I see one. The back of your accelerating car
I love fascistically. Friend,
put your teeth on the table. Friend,
would you leave me in the jungle without a rag
to dance to? Why drop me at the corner
of nothing and nothing, my tongue lolling?

Joel Lipman
Translitic from Julián del Casal's "A un amigo"

PETER HUTTINGER

PENS AND PENCILS

Scripto pens and pencils
Are essential to all writing
Does not require stencils
More personal than typing

Both are used in twain
While the sky is blue
Or perhaps heavy rain
One plus one equals two

Pencils and pens
Verbally not talk
Can't be used by hens
But most animals walk

They can't be used by wrens
Who fly sky high
They are never in pens
One can always try

Can be purchased at the variety store
Five plus five equals ten
Frequently give me more
Either by women or men

The silent writing pen
Always as a prayer
While no educational yen
Has no visible hair

Said pen to t'other
Do you enjoy writing?
Be careful don't smother
Or try physical prize fighting.

Ernest Noyes Brookings

I am not your puppet. Take your hand from up my skirt.
There is no welcome there for you grim ventriloquist.

unloaded a trailer of hangers for breakfast – went out on an afternoon ticket for five tearing down pyrobrick walls in a dusty basement full of damaged christmas trinkets, decorations, flannel flags from different states, boxes of old invoices

put the headed half of smashed porcelain saint in a lightbulb cage with a stalk of tiny plastic bananas, backscratcher skeleton hand, bride, and half a blond mermaid, the burnt remainder of an old flag on a stick

headless jesus in a dead refrigerator with a decoy duck in the freezer disemboweled fuse box black wires hanging photo of someones son suspended on the prongs of a kitchen fork

mildewed nudist magazine "they all sat down to eat"

S. Gustav Hägglund

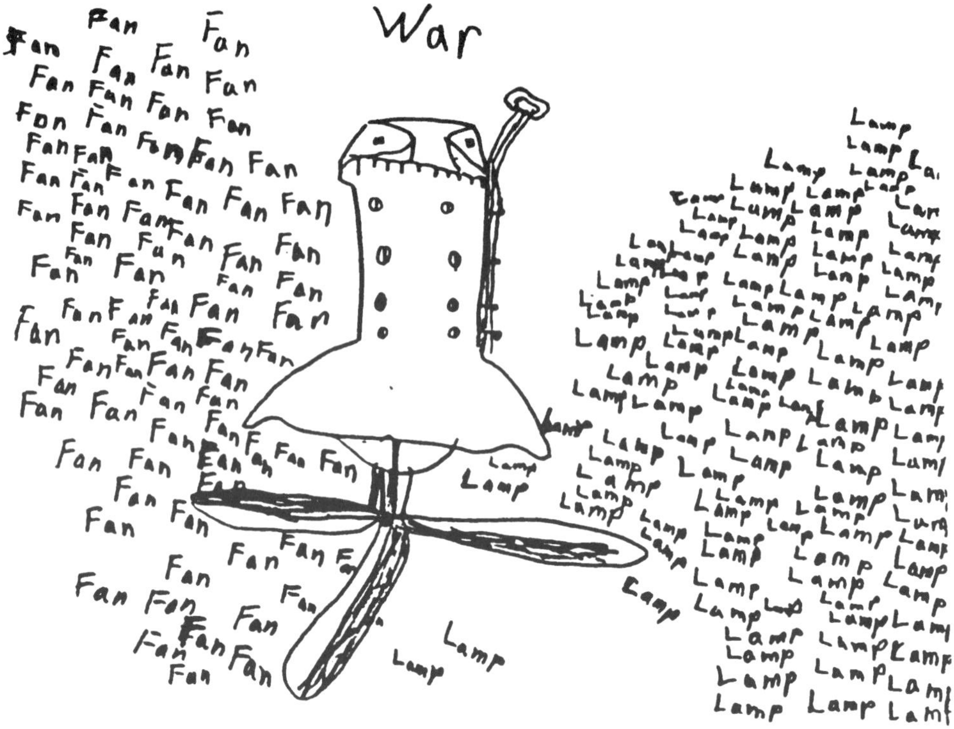

Hosea Frank

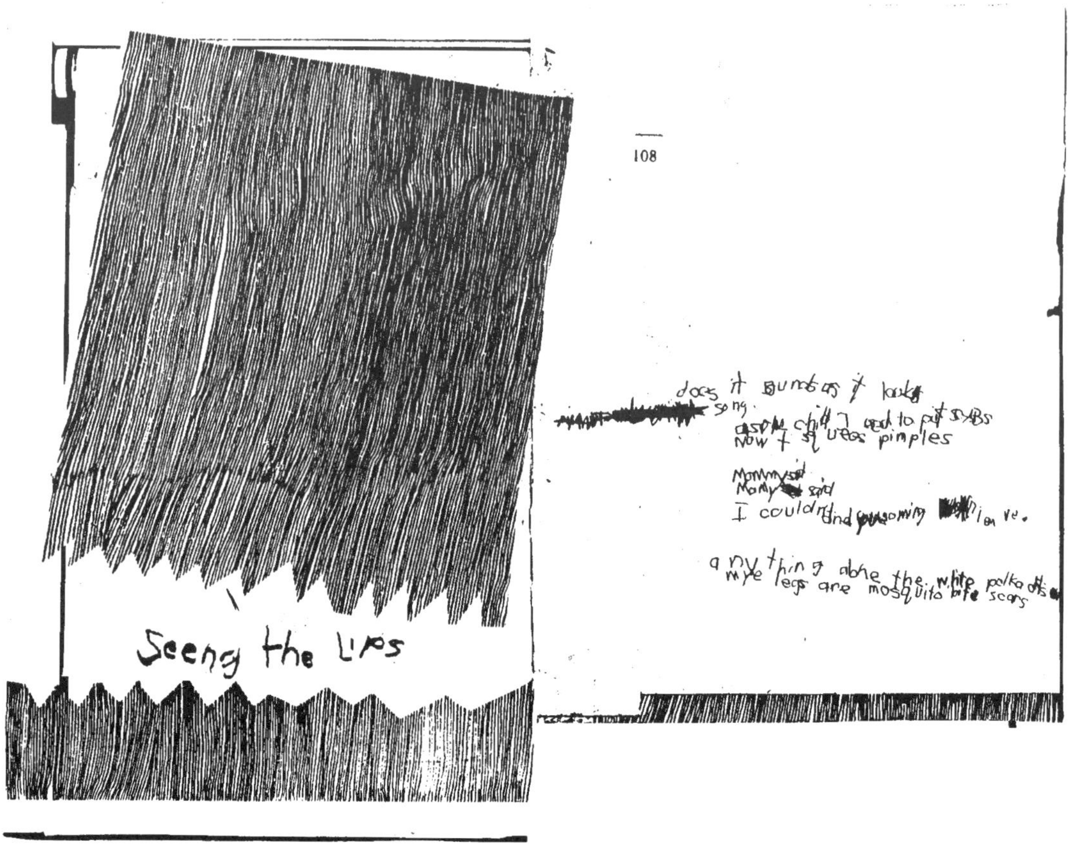

Vicky Mansoor

DAVI DET HOMPSON DEFINES JOHN M. BENNETT'S WORDS

Blunker – noun, one who blunks. A blunker is a person who presses large dimples into car doors and fenders with a foot or knee.

The – The Thes were a primitive tribe living on the southeastern shore of what is now Great Britain. Named after a characteristic sound made whenever they pointed to objects.

Histic – A permanent open boil-like sore that is used by East Indian gurus to absorb all of the body's ailments into one place. Usually induced in an out-of-sight area; for example, on the inner side of a knee or under the hair.

Lumberate – To turn over in one's mind, to consider large, formless concepts of contemporary and historical importance without conclusion. Although usually conducted without acknowledgement, a conscious episode of lumberation can be triggered by a minor occurrence such as the crack between a store window's dummy's hand and wrist or a TV news reporter staring into the camera as he waits for a pre-recorded message.

Gaster – The plastic pull-up tip on a white glue or liquid detergent bottle that opens and closes the spout.

JOHN M. BENNETT DEFINES DAVI DET HOMPSON'S WORDS

Noggle – n. cranial drain hose, used after surgery. v. to jostle a person's hoses; i.e., to confuse.

Wamp – n. viscous ooze on basement walls. v. (colloq.) to spit on a person's pants.

Sucigate – v. to walk with the knees turned out and slumping to the right or left with each step; applied to ambitious civil servants.

Fluch – adj. used to indicate a stopped-up toilet that is full to the brim with fecal matter, as in "a fluch toilet". v. to fill with fecal matter.

Davi Det Hompson & John M. Bennett

THE PHOTOGRAPHED HOUSE

The skin of her face had been burned. As I walked the steps leading to their house I dared look at her grimace of pain felt in that first terrible searing; now permanently stretched from temple to jaw.

Inside the house *The Seven Samurai* had begun. On the floor a cockroach was scratching toward me, touching its way from table to chair leg, its stealth betrayed by the television's blue-grey light. I asked, "Are you angry?" She answered, "Yes", then said again, "Yes I am." "Do you imagine that you will ever be more at ease than you are now?"

She shifted her eyes for a long moment to the collection of snap-shots hung above the dresser. "Perhaps, but I hope not. My anger is a document of that other life."

We gathered our things, said goodbye then waited as he closed the house; pulling shut curtains, tightening faucets and stringing trip-wire alarms across the thresholds.

Davi Det Hompson

13427 POEMES METAPHYSIQUES. POEME N° 84

HOT-DOG
CHICHI
PIZZA

DEJA FAIT

Julien Blaine

ASLEEP AT THE WHEEL

He'll be standing high on a ladder
in his fingertips splinters a
wind pulling at his back he'll be
looking through the glass he'll
see an empty table a chair whirling before it a
column of smoke standing above the empty boards

He's crouching in a room with
4 black walls he stares to the north he
sees a concrete tree with
arms hanging from the leaves he
stares to the east: a wall of ice with
hands glinting behind the surface he's
whirling to the west he sees a hole with
lights and shouting deep inside it; to the
south to the south he sees a giant chair
burning, a dog sleeping and twitching beneath it

He was sleeping he was
pressing his butt in the sofa he was
clawing in his dream at the ceiling he was
trying to wake he was
seeing a lurching highway
holes and cracks speeding beneath him

John M. Bennett

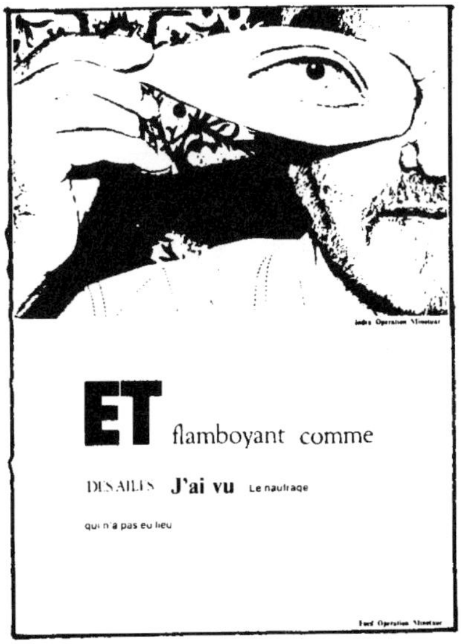

Charles Henri Ford & Indra

Dream-

policemen and red searchlights.

RED WIND

the night into small strips

RED WIND

I reached in far enough
in past me like a wave.

the trees shook
in my fingers

S. Gustav Hägglund

from THE SINO-KOREAN TRANSLATIONS

make one's blood
the blood

a law violation

sleep

disturb the
the idea

live in
3 unities

jwcurry/Mark Laba

OLD GUY LIMPING

Old guy limping slightly was walking his way barefoot through the broken glass. Every now and then he yanked a foot from the cement hard and hopped to the curb where he'd sit awkwardly and lift a leg across the other knee.

When he picked the shred of glass from the tough black skin, a speck of drool would spill from the left side of the sweet mouth small and he'd peer curiously at that dot of blood.

Then in a little, he came to a telephone pole and went past a bit, stopped and turned back. He called to me.

And we looked at that wood thing tall and straight. We looked where knots were bellybuttons of old limbs that used to stretch out with green and autumn gold. Now only a few had even creosote to keep them from rotting all and falling down with wire veins which would make things unwhite.

We walked together wondering why the smell of wine hugged so tightly around those old-time trees.

Paul Weinman

VENUS IN TRANSIT

pyramids of meat lighter than gold
afloat in the northernmost hemisphere
where the gods gagging on orbital reflex
wager for last kisses
her circles burn right through metal
I am reduced to gibbering ash in her eyes
the here and now of all cyprus
envelopes me with contrary urges
I send signals to the united states
with magnets that draw the maps from their style
confusion beautiful riots of sleep
where faces promiscuously exchanged
assume the divine dimension!
there is more water than ever before
the caves of ajanta light up with her salt
organisms of multiple waists and hips
enormous fluid beings emerging from stone
this planet of endless promiscuity!

inspiration of sand and glass
the pointless epic of fire gongs and flutes
what wild untamed beasts are singed in their hair
by this raving illusion
my third eye pivots in the Wood
and the number thirty three repeats itself
in cymbals of urgent catastrophe!

Ivan Argüelles

My cat dusunt have
vere Good teeth
at all thae are blude
and grae but
thae are shrpe
las nite I stuck
my tuing at hem
he snift it and
then likt it. I told
mie Mom se
sed ewwww!

William E. Bennett

BITING THE BRICK

"Biting biting" he shouts in front of the
supphose display a man in a flat white hat
is running at him an
aeresol spraycan slapping at his waist

No-Boy was pulling bricks from the mud and watching his
nails splinter and bleed on the
stuckon jags of cement
he feels the heavy blue sky on his back he's
trying to lurch himself and the
bricks upright against it

He'll be brooding in the bathtub he'll
be rising in his face he'll
be turning his fixed stare he'll
be heading again at the landfill
dragging his feet and smell to the
mud and filled up place of running water

"No-Boy No-Boy" he mutters over and over stalking
down the street; at the drugstore, can't
find the shoelaces, hears
the rain explode outside a
flopping in his belly he wants to
vomit and be falling sleeping in the
river surging through the parkinglot

A single tooth sticks from between his lips
"It's Brick" he thinks
lifting the dark lumpy rectangle to his mouth

John M. Bennett

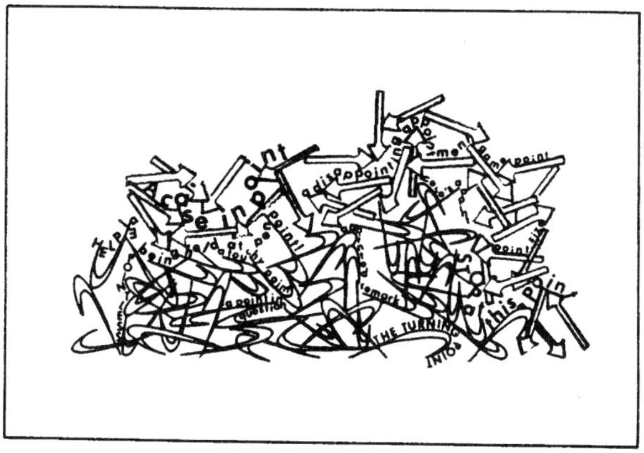

Marilyn R. Rosenberg

ACK'S WACKS
a column of gastropodal Insight.

"ANDY JAWS AND THE GUMP"

(Dateline – Austin, Texas – 15/6/83)

The Austin Comedy Workshop featured a very interesting act the other night—Andy Jaws and The Gump—and we made a point of driving the seventy–some–odd miles to catch it. Andy Jaws and The Gump interested us because of what Paul LaFaith, a medical journalist in Florida, had written about them several years ago in THE OTHER ROOM, a magazine that makes a specialty of reporting on "new cults, alternate states of existence, mutations and strange agents," as the magazine's masthead always puts it. The LaFaith article, titled "The New Dummyism," began with a survey of the then growing number of performers who were electing to have themselves surgically altered to resemble Elvis, Janis Joplin, and Jackie Kennedy. "The more extreme side of all this," wrote LaFaith, "is that last month a man who calls himself Andy Jaws actually had one of his hands surgically altered into a tiny head, complete with face. Andy Jaws is a ventriloquist, you see, and his hand-head, built mostly out of hip fat, sports an especially mobile mouth, sockets for glass eyes, even moveable skin flaps for eye-lids. A deluxe job—and judging from the medical photos I saw at the hospital, I'd venture to say that once on stage and dressed up like Charlie McCarthy, the head (which Andy bills as "The Gump") could pass for the genuine article; although close to and without the glass eyes, it looked less like a face than it did a Chinese concubine's foot, one fresh from the bindings, a truly unsettling sight. Hair had been transplanted, too, but that looked to be sparse and just coming in. The interesting thing to speculate on, is Andy's mental states, particularly as time goes by, now that he has his little pal always there at the end of his wrist to talk to... and do things with."

To describe the act itself as we caught it the other night at the Comedy Workshop. Well, neither LaFaith's advance warning nor the five or six gin fizzes that we got behind early on at our table down close to ringside had prepared us for the reality of Andy Jaws and The Gump. Andy Jaws has red hair for one thing, the kind that goes with very pale skin and lashes—so does the Gump, grown out, in the little head's case, into a kind of modified, yarny fright-wig. A small yellow bow-tie sewn to the ventriloquist's sleeve was the only attempt to outfit or costume The Gump, yet chattering and bobbing there in the blue spotlight, The Gump's presence quickly established itself, and it soon became difficult not to think of the altered hand (or head) as a separate entity. The act started routinely enough. Andy Jaws, repeatedly shoving The Gump down toward his fly, seemed poised to do low crotch jokes all night. After a good deal of inane patter, the pair wrangled their way into an off-key duet, something called "I Wonder Who's Kissing Her Whatchamacallit?"—all, all commonplace. Then, in a moment of extraordinary transition, it was as though the Gump were speaking for the first time. "All right, now, you go away, Andy," said The Gump, "and *I'll* talk." The ventriloquist's head was bowed, as if in trance; the audience, hushed, had entered into a blue midnight space; and we heard, from deep in a place of our own, a voice saying "Hello, gang." It was a feminine voice, unmistakably. "Hello, gang," it began in a young, rather querulous nasal tone, which from the sound of it was no stranger to the bathroom medicine cabinet where the prescription pills and capsules live. But the monologue that followed was too mysterious an organism to be dissected, or even recalled very precisely. Here, then, is the best we can do at reconstructing the essence of it:

"Hello, gang. I'm Mrs Cookie. Annie Cookie. This is my husband Andy Cookie, who works six days a week at Calico Instruments, Inc. He's into a transition phase at work. This is our little one, Evelyn-Morgan. She's into the 'into everything!' stage of development. We have many television sets and microwaves and labor-saving gadgets. We're the Cookie Family. We love to drive from one shopping place to another. But"—(here the voice seemed to take on a special hectic excitement)—"beware of the scarlet scarecrow and the dancing blue woman and the shaggy man. Relax not your vigilance against them for even a second. *Revelation 2:22.* Oh, how it frets my heart to think about them. Especially that nasty shaggy man. But we should always remain pleased with the good things we have. Our neighbors have a house on the lake. It is great summer excitement. Andy is looking for a new project at work. Evelyn-Morgan loved her first swim. Last Friday, we thought we saw the shaggy man lurking in the mild sunshine outside the shopping center. But our friend the china Snoopy dog appeared just in time to drive him away. It was as if no time had passed. Back at the house again, Andy went out to jog around the golf-links; Evelyn-Morgan enjoyed a snack of peanut butter and crackers; and I passed the late afternoon hours crumbling potato chips to go on top of the Tuna Casserole Supreme for our young adult's prayer group. Well, that's the news from this neck of the woods. It's wonderful to have air conditioning. Remember, don't toss out your old panty hose—you can make pillows, toys, flowers, even a rug. One more little item. Another little Cookie is on the way. ETA January 2nd. Yes, this was planned and we are delighted. Look around. More and more of us every day. Goodbye. See you real soon," the voice said to the Comedy Workshop audience. ("See you real soon," echoed the audience.)

That is the gist of it. We have no doubt we've omitted a lot, but this queer hypnotic monologue left us so groggy—the side of our head buzzing like a flounder—that it was several minutes before we even realized that Andy Jaws and The Gump were off the stage. Later, at a crowded after-the-show party, the dolorous, sinister implications of the thing struck us as we stood and watched Andy Jaws, his hand now covered in a black silk bag, cavorting and mixing and having the time of his life. He did not touch a drop of booze and yet he looked ready to wear a lampshade and kick over the cake. We have since wondered why he should look so happy, so much the best-integrated, most fulfilled American personality we have encountered in years.

Al Ackerman

The Little Dogs Laughed to See Such Lunacy

A COLUMN OF HIGH FINANCE AND DECORUM BY DR AL ACKERMAN

"Dear Dr Al: I've heard that back in the mid-60s your friends called you "The Crab." I wish you'd fill us in on how this nickname came about, if it isn't too embarrassing," writes a reader from Bethlehem, Pa.

This is undoubtedly a widespread longing. But in order to fill you in on how I came to be called "The Crab," I have to first fill you in on how one summer I was taking a two week vacation from my regular hospital job and I got the idea that it might make an interesting experiment to go around town putting in bogus job applications, a routine that consisted of me scanning the help wanted columns until I found a dismal-sounding job about which I knew absolutely nothing, and then going right in and applying for it under an assumed name, which seemed preferable to using my own because it gave me a chance to see if anybody remembered "Harry Emerson Fosdick" or "Friederich Engels," though as it turned out they didn't even remember "Charles Starkweather," and nobody ever knew me for an imposter. I also made it a big point at each office I visited (this was one of the prime factors in my experiment) to personally exhibit different types of weird, shabby and inappropriate behaviour.

I started out by answering an ad for "Price Change Clerk for Wholesale Plumbing Supply—must know 10 key calculator." This seemed made to order for my first venture into the realm of bogus job hunting because I was completely in the dark as to what a price change clerk might be, and I knew no more about the 10 key calculator than does Emily Fusselman's rabbit. A rather humorless woman who looked a little like Mrs Tucker does on the lard cans and was the wife of the plumbing store owner interviewed me. Grudgingly she handed me a pencil and a few flimsy yellow forms to fill out and pointed me to a chair in the corner, and then proceeded to give me the double-o with a dismay that was clear and unalloyed. Mostly because the blue seer sucker suit I was wearing on that sweltering day hadn't been cleaned or pressed since Christmas and I had gone three days without a shave or bath especially for the occasion. I'd also been careful to drink half a pint of fine Four Roses Whiskey before entering the establishment, and I reeked. I could feel her eyeing my filthy collar and stubbly jowls and wrinkling her nose at the essence of Four Roses that came rolling off me at every breath, as from a pungent old cork. I spent a long, long time like that, hunched over the simple yellow forms, fumbling with my pencil, wheezing and sweating and mopping my face, giving every indication that if I managed to keep from passing out cold on the floor, it would be a real victory. Pretty soon the plumbing lady came over and asked me if I was alright. "You don't look so good, Mr Voltaire," she said. "I can't think of how you spell Travis County," I said. "Oh," she said. "Well, maybe you should come back another time when you're feeling better—"I breathed on her some more and said, "It's just that these ulcers I get on my leg make it hard to concentrate and I think that must be what's hanging me up now because I started getting a big one last night and it's been draining on me all morning." She looked at my legs and stepped back. On this note the interview pretty well concluded, and I managed to control myself until I got out of the building.

The name I gave to this particular routine was "The Secret Drinker" and the reactions it elicited interested me to such an extent that I spent the next few days experimenting and trying out different variations on it. For example, at the offices of Church's Chicken, where I applied for the position of "Manager Trainee" under the name of "Fulton J. Sheen", an honest but inveterate beer drinker, I had to get up twice to ask the secretary for more paper because it was taking a lot of space to list all of "Fulton J's" arrests and hospitalizations. But I hung in there, and the secretary's expression when she finally got a load of this strange and terrible human document was my reward. A day or so later at a northside blueprint firm with an immediate opening for "Civil Draftsman—min. 5 years experience," I showed up with an enormous purple wine stain down my front that was still wet and, having knocked into a couple of chairs on my way up to the receptionist's desk, was quickly told that the civil drafting position had *just* been filled. You could have knocked me down with a hammer. "Well," I said, throwing my eyes wildly around the office, "then do you need a civil draftsman?" (I didn't get that job, either.) Another company downtown wanted "Salesman For Manufactured House Goods," and by using the name "Felix Frankfurter," along with a fixed smile and fairly clean clothes, I actually made it past the receptionist and had a short interview with the company sales manager, a Mr Dix. He was a rather spiritless-looking but not unsympathetic character and things didn't go too badly at first. But there was no way to hide the deep thirst that raged inside me (or inside "Felix") and before long I fell off the subject of manufactured house goods and into a fervid rambling disquistition on my fondness for all sorts of hot mulled rum drinks. Mr Dix, unable to ignore these conspicuous warning signs, sat through about five minutes of this and then eased me out of his office. "Honey," I told him at the door, "remember to sweeten the rum drink with six tablespoons of honey!" He promised he would.

Hard by. In most of the personnel offices in this country there seems to be at least a tenuous rule in effect prohibiting the staff from attempting to hurt the prospective applicants by physical means. But there is no law against low psychology and many humiliating tricks are employed successfully to make the job hunter feel like a little gob of spit. So it was a heady sensation indeed for me to feel that I was, at least for the moment, turning the tables on this age-old vassalage, and I was coming out of these encounters higher than a kite, already leaping ahead in my mind to the next office and concocting new routines right and left.

"The Shouter," "The Aggrieved Epileptic," "Active T.B.," "The Lonely Nosepicker of Avalon," "Freaky Deaky." I had hopes I might try out each and every one of these promising routines before my two week vacation was up, but this was not to be, and as it worked out, I only got to spring "The Shouter" on them. This was at a downtown savings and loan where the Assistant Manager, who resembled Ken (of Ken and Barbie fame) and wore lavender-tinted aviators and white suede loafers with little gold links on them, called me into his office after an interminable wait and interviewed me for the position of "Retail Banking Specialist." I was wearing my best suit and had spruced myself up considerably for this one. Under the name of "Benedict 'Dutch' Spinoza," I answered his questions in a nebulous way, making sure that with every sentence I uttered my voice crept up the scale and became louder. Toward the end I was frankly shouting. This alarming and crackbrained increase in volume was accomplished in such gradual stages that I don't think he was ever precisely aware of what was going on or even where we'd left the tracks. I might have kept it up indefinitely until my voice failed or I burst a blood vessel, but the mystified, fidgety, discomfited look on his face was too much for me and I lost it. Laughing hysterically like a hyena I had to jump up and run out of there fast.

That was when it happened. Outside on the street, my own gales of hilarity distracted me so that I stepped right in the path of an oncoming truck and got clipped. I wound up with a mild concussion and two broken arms. (Editors' Note: The awful implacable gods of mercantile are not lightly mocked.)

And so with a cast on each arm bent at the elbows and crooked out in front of me awkwardly that way for the next couple of months, it was inevitable that my friends should take to calling me "The Crab".

Al Ackerman

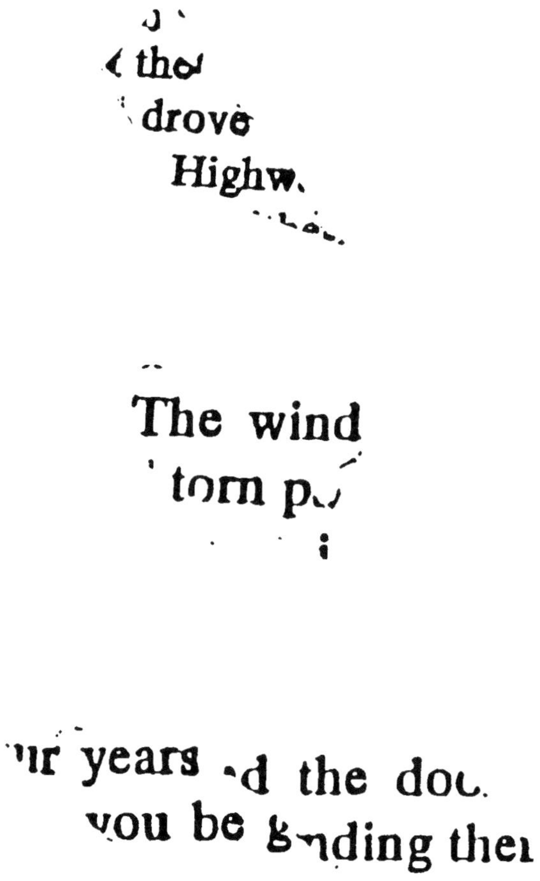

S. Gustav Hägglund

DR. D.
AND THE CURSE OF THE BIRD IN SPACE
A NEW LOOK FOR A NEW TIME
PREFORMED IN THE ALL NEW
3-D
INDIA INK TECHNIQUE THAT WILL MAKE YOU THINK TWICE!
ALL
EVER WANTED!!
HMMM PLAN, PLAN, MUTTER, GUF, GRIPE...
LOOKS LIKE THE DR IS O.T.R.!!
I MUST FIND OUT HOW LOW THEY WILL GO! I MUST KNOW THE LIMITS!
AND YET IN DOING SO, I MUST NOT BE "ARTFUL" THERE MUST BE NO CONTENT! NO REWARD!
PAINTED YOURSELF IN TO A CORNER DR?
NO WAY! THE PUBLIC WILL COME THROUGH FOR ME!
WHY ELSE DO IT?
??
DR. D.
THEY ALWAYS HAVE BEFORE
WHATA GUY!

John Adams

ANIMALS - male urination performance text for video

by Michael Basinski

HORSE

RHINOSAROUS

GOAT

HIPPO

PYTHON

BULL

STALION

BULL

SHARK

WHALE

ELEPHANT

TIGER

LION

EAGLE

RAM

GORILLA

ALLIGATOR

Horse

Bull

BISON

Buffalo

BUFFALO

BUFFALO

Goat

Lamb

chicken duck

pony

frog

pollywog

insect

parameciem

amebas

ameba ameba ameba

ameba

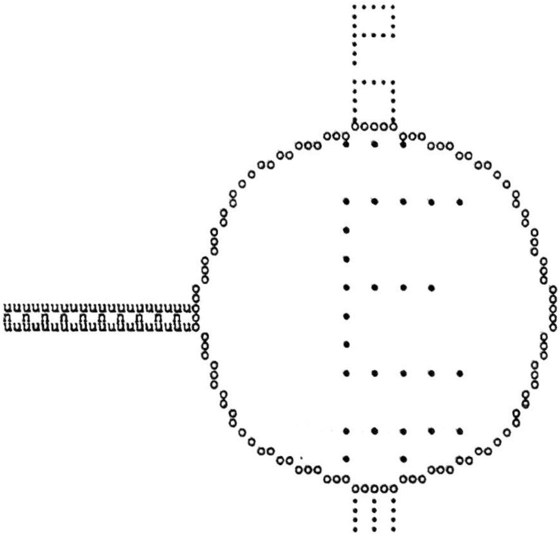

Karl Kempton

Ack's Wack's
a dept of high Political analysis

"THE JIGGLING MEN MYSTERY"

Cornel Petey owns and operates a yellow suitcase of the stand-up variety that he uses to sell his many magic and novelty items out of, and for twenty-two years he has been, in his own words, "pitching the woo" out of doorways along Houston Street in downtown San Antonio, Texas—or, on days when the cops seem inclined to hassle him, "adjooring" around the corner to some less conspicuous alleyway. So when Ralph "$50,000 Party" Delgado, the director of the highly successful charity organization "Parties For Orphans", needed something special last week in the way of favors to pass out at an orphan's Halloween party he was hosting, he called upon Mr Petey, whom he introduced to me as "the famed novelty salesman."

The man we were meeting looked like a swarthy and somewhat sawed-off Slim Whitman, and he was got up in an unobtrusive ensemble of sharkskin jacket, porkpie hat, cotton slacks, and wide napkin tie secured by a small gold clip, in various shades of maroon-and-gray, except for the tie which was lime green and featured giant sea horses athwart tumbling coxcombs. Mr Petey's voice reminds you of George Burns, and his way of looking you over without ever quite seeming to focus his eyes is shrewd and certainly a good reminder that, as Algis Budrys once remarked, you may never be educated enough or find the right attitude in time. Ralph "$50,000 Party" Delgado had scheduled a meeting with Mr Petey for late Saturday morning coffee at Shoop's, a cafe specializing in seafood and something called the "Shoop Salad" (lettuce and Thousand Island, from the looks of it), that is patronized chiefly by people who don't want to eat at the Grayhound Station across the street, and Mr Petey slithered in from his room at the Ace Hotel two blocks away, which is his current home base, lugging a yellow tin suitcase about four feet square and ten inches deep, which he set up next to our table on battered metal legs that unfolded out of the bottom, like an ironing board or a tv tray—a suitcase containing his wares. Opened, it looked like the bargain bin at Bernie's Fun 'N Magic Shop, on Commerce Street. On top, the suitcase held a row of flat, blue-and-white cardboard men, each about twelve inches high with accordian-pleated crepe-paper arms and legs colored bright day-glo orange; Mr Petey told us this was his line of famed "jiggling men," and gave us a little speech about how when you set the men up and activated them in a certain way (a patented secret that would be fully explained in the instruction pamphlet that accompanies each and every doll sold) the things actually took life and danced or jiggled of their own accord, completely without wires or any other "hidden apparatus." There was a pause, during which Ralph "$50,000 Party" Delgado, hulking, oily, and saturnine, studied the now quiescent jiggling men through narrowed eyes, as though trying to decide how best to frame some question that was bothering him, while his fork continued to toy among the ruins of his "Shoop Salad" and the seconds lengthened into minutes and I (and, I assume, Mr Petey also) began to feel discomfited and slightly embarrassed by his silence. As Mr Petey manipulated the pleated arms on one of his dolls to demonstrate its suppleness and fine workmanship (and in response to Ralph's less than cordial demeanor), I cleared my throat and attempted to say something friendly and inconsequential to relieve the tension—something about how I'd always wondered what it was that made the little men jiggle—but it was obvious to me, from the way Mr Petey was fidgeting, that Ralph's silence was casing a definite pall. It depressed me no end to find things deteriorating like this, because, in point of fact, if it hadn't been for the embarrassment I was feeling, I would more than have welcomed a chance to find out how the jiggling men worked, for this was something that had intrigued and puzzled me for years, ever since the day in 1952 when my father had taken me downtown for a new pair of Red Goose shoes and we had glimpsed one of the fabled dolls dancing and jiggling in a doorway next to the shoe store. That day had marked the beginning of my fascination with the mystery of the jiggling men. When my father had refused to shell out four bits for one of the things and the vendor (not Mr Petey but surely a distant cousin of Mr Petey's) had shown signs of folding up his suitcase and moving on, I gave way utterly to the *angst* of the moment, and my screams in a matter of minutes proved sufficient to draw a fair-sized crowd and send the poor peddler scuttling down the street with his suitcase clutched under his arm, increasing to full-blown hysterics once I really got going; and, truth to tell, I wound up going considerably beyond hysterics, actually falling on my father's feet, punching, kicking, flailing, slobbering, writhing, moaning, howling, drooling, choking, barking, sobbing, keening, convulsing, and biting my father's ankles.

"You bit your father a half dozen times on the ankles while you were like that, and then you shifted your grip and bit him on the fleshy part of the calf," my mother would say, recalling the incident in later years. "I was afraid we were going to have to have you committed, but Dr Miller said to just put you in your room and keep an eye on you. The whole month you were screaming we were living in that awful post-war housing with the pasteboard walls so you kept us in dutch something awful with the neighbors. You would yell and try to bite anybody that went near you. We had to tell everybody you had scarlet fever."

My grandmother had been listening to my mother's comments. "At the risk of hurting your feelings, Albert, I have to say you wet the bed and carried on like a fiend," she said.

Recalling the shame and darkness of those years (and thrown off stride by Ralph's brooding silence), I heard myself asking Mr Petey if he had ever felt the uncontrollable urge to take his thumb and mash out a pigeon's eyes. Mr Petey looked at me and said, "Fuck, no. Why? Have you?", glancing uneasily from me to Ralph and back again. Among the many desires I have entertained (I found myself telling Mr Petey) are "Pigeon Punching," "Bicycle Sniffing," "Bread Braiding," "Toupé Fondling," and a number of urges I call the How-can-I-tell-you type urge. Over a period ranging from my early sorrow at missing out on owning a jiggling man through that of my later dismissals from several military academies, I entertained a whole series of desires centering on the Velo Benzedrine Inhaler. In those days, neither the Army nor the Navy would touch me, because when it came to enlisting a self-confessed Velo freak the Vietnam conflict had not yet reached the stage where these branches of the armed services were grabbing up anything that breathed or moved. In 1972, I clipped a photo of a medical diploma out of the AMA Digest, filled it in with a ballpoint pen, hung it up and opened a small mail-order business specializing in "sight-unseen" cancer cures. Since then, repeated failures and a lot of angry mail from relatives of patients had given me new perspective and helped calm me down to the point where I could now sit in a cheap restaurant and keep most of my clothes on. "And so I feel that by next year I will be far enough along to drink from a cup and apply for a driver's license," I told Mr Petey, doing my best to keep things upbeat. Meanwhile, Ralph's behavior had grown increasingly bizarre.

"My watch," he muttered, breaking his long silence at last, and staring hard at Mr Petey. "Why did you steal my watch, Aunt Linda? WHY?"

Was it this—or was it the way Ralph had scrunched down in his chair until just his eyes were peering over the edge of his plate at us that caused Mr Petey to jump up and run out of the cafe with his suitcase clutched under his arm?

There was no time to wonder. At this point the door to the kitchen burst open and out came the cook and his three assistants, bread sticks up their nostrils. They broke into song, and a highly nasal version of "The Star Spangled Banner" rent the air. What horror! When next I knew, I was out on the sidewalk running for my life with Ralph clutched under my arm.

"Maybe I shouldn't have swallowed a whole bottle of saccharine tablets after breakfast this morning," Ralph admitted later that afternoon when I put him down under a bench in the park. Which explained a good deal about his hopped-up behavior at the table but in no way consoled me. For once again I had missed my chance to learn the secret of the jiggling men. *Oh, God in heaven! How long must I wait? How many more pigeons must die beneath my thumbs before I learn the secret?!*

(And so on. This is being written on Election Day, and my first idea was to try to convey something of the feeling, ineffable and dismal and all at sea, that comes stealing over me when I contemplate the current political scene and what is being wrought. Well, turns out this parable of the jiggling men, wherein I seem to find myself sitting in a bad restaurant as if in a dream, with a shady street vendor staring at me in dismay, and all sorts of rubbishy, outlandish vapors and notions coursing through my brain, while across the table a friend goes insane on saccharine and everybody else pokes bread sticks up their nose and gets patriotic—turns out this pale, half-ass approximation was as close as I could come. In other words, close but no cigar.)

Al Ackerman

Vittore Baroni

NOON

the spittoon was peerless, splashing the immense sobbing
volcano with platonic greetings. its feeble lantern
launched the mutant up the gushing ladder, lending compassion
to the jostling protozoan that was profaning the opium
navy. precaution moaned in its waspish lotus, honing the
saucy membrane to a radiant minaret. a parakeet was
muttering gauze flowers to all the spastic nuggets. it
was hungry for oxides and love.

Bob Heman

TOILETSEAT

I was rubbing my thighs with toiletseat to the
floor I was nailing a toiletseat
standing on a toiletseat I was flailing at the
ants on the ceiling I was spinning in the
eye of a toiletseat wiping on the
toiletseat a sausage I was trying to
open the toiletseat make a door of the
toiletseat I slapped the toiletseat against the
window was biting and kicking the toiletseat hurling my
change at the toiletseat I lowered over my
head the toiletseat and ran to the drugstore,
shouted DOCTOR at the fleeing clerks; I was
hiding in the trashbin I was
hugging the seat under my shirt I was
hoping it would guide me, be flushing the dark, be a
boat and a mirror and a headlight

SHIRT

I was shrugging my shirt falling in a
muddy hole in my shirt I was reaching for a
doorknob in my shirt sleeping my shirt in a
car as it veered at the berm I was boiling and
folding my shirt I was spitting, chewing
wiping my feet on my shirt I was shirting my
duty streaking my shirt in the parkinglot on
Thursday I took my shirt to a bowling alley and
pinned and balled my shirt my shirt was
bulging ripped over the back of a chair I was
throwing coffdrops at my shirt putting in the
pocket of my shirt a handfull of
nails and a rubber ant I was throwing the
shirtdressed chair into the street where a
garbage truck chuffed and smoked I was
napping in my shirtless skin and a
dream shirted my head it was undershirts polishing a shovel

John M. Bennett

LA CABEZA

En el mes de febrero decapitaron al rebelde Zelarrayán, sin apelación, por orden del Restaurador de las Leyes. Varios días estuvo expuesta la cabeza en el patio de su casa, en Palermo, sobre un áspero mantel de la curia.

La hija del robusto tirano, Manuelita, la vio rebotar sin fortuna como una pelota y, alarmada, pidío llorando que la sacaran del corredor adonde había sido empujada.

Con lenta obediencia, Rosas tomó la cabeza con sus dedos y la depositó sobre una mesa, dentro del calabozo de Céspedes y de otro rebelde, Bidasari. A un edecán se le dio la orden de hacer cumplir el pedido, pero de un modo más ilustre. Céspedes y Bidasari debían permanecer hincados, con la barbilla pegada a la mesa, mirando fijamente la cabeza de Zelarrayán. Y así muchas horas, a la luz de una cruz y una bujía.

Con el tiempo la cabeza se quebró en dos y se deshizo en polvo fino. Los prisioneros habían tolerado con decoro la penuria: Se pusieron de pie y una leve sonrisa los alumbró.

Pero le deslizaron otra cabeza, con los ojos tenazmente vivos, como carbúnculos. Céspedes y Bidasari volvieron a su ostensorio. Y esta vez, fabulosamente, la cabeza se arrugó y se volvió harina negra. Algunos minutos fueron interrumpidos por el paso de batallones. Se escuchaban bombas de fiesta, y en los barrios lejanos quemaron petardos.

Después llegaron cabezas sin pellejo, mascadas por los cerdos. Y cabezas con huellas de sable o pisadas por bueyes. Cabezas de niños, sin ojos, con los cabellos como helechos mojados . . . Milgrosamente, Céspedes y Bidasari, iban venciendo los peligros que rápidamente se les presentaban. Así, una y otra vez, bajo pena de muerte, mientras se oía el paso de los batallones, y después el silencio, a la luz de una cruz y una bujía.

Armado Zárate

fill in
ing
kill with hunger

TAR
  TAR
    TAR
      TAR

jwcurry

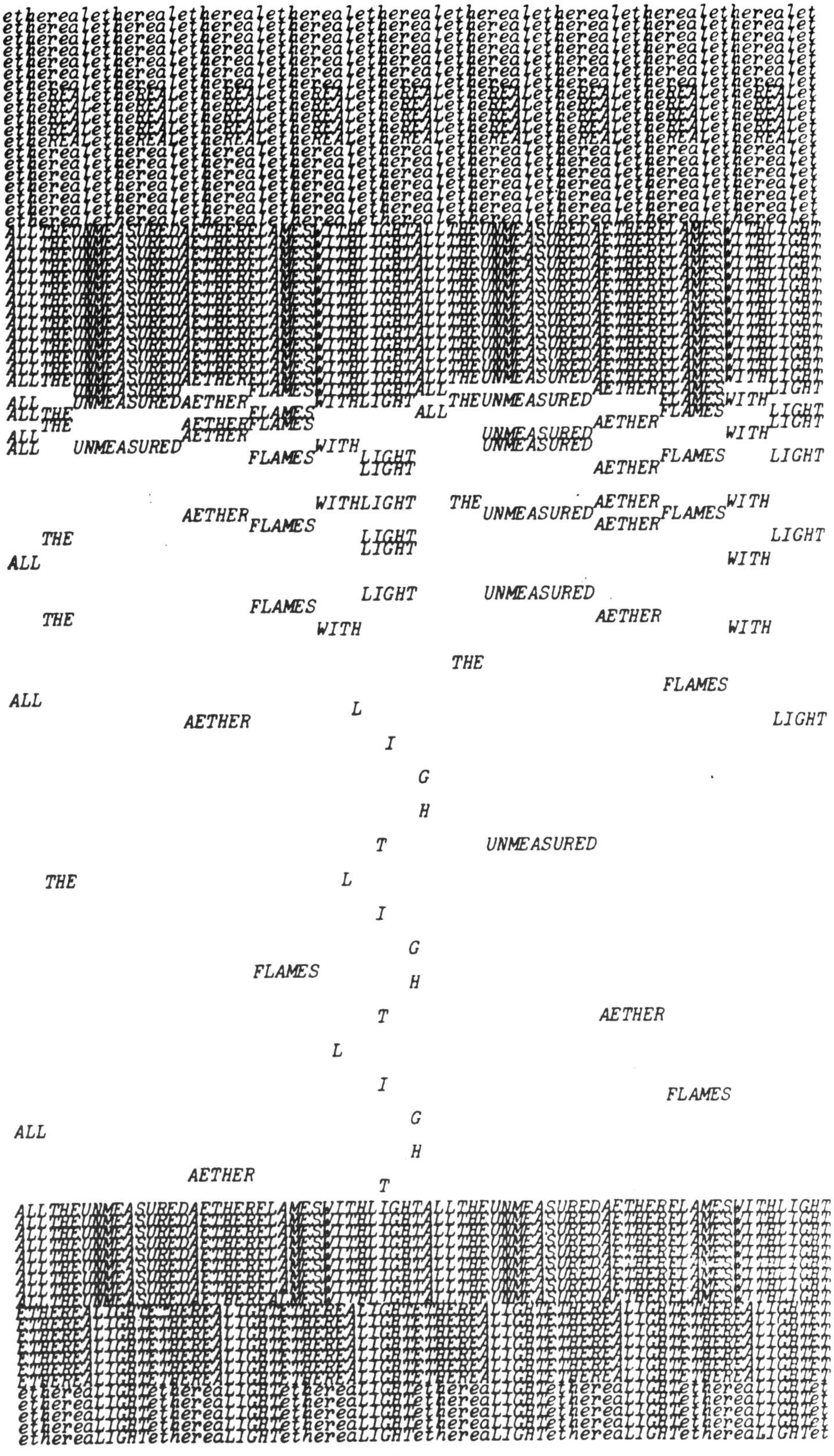

Paula Claire

ACK'S WACKS
A Column Of Anatomical
Diminuendo

When four readers of this magazine, one right after another, sent letters and complimented me on my most recent column I knew there must be something wrong. Nowdays one complimentary letter is unusual, four in a row are almost frightening. It quickly became apparent that the letter writers were seriously off-base, not to say totally deluded. Their letters, for one thing, seemed to assume that my column had been about macaroni—"the best —— article on macaroni that I have ever come across," as one reader put it. Feeling nervous I reread the column in question (as far as I knew, my article had been about Cornel Petey the famed novelty salesman) to see if I could uncover any mention of macaroni and found only a passing reference to bread sticks which, though they are a staple in many pasta joints, was to my mind insufficient grounds for misinterpretation or confusion of this magnitude, Well, my friends, I think that this little episode points up once again what happens when any sizable portion of the reading audience falls victim to the ravages of "false memory," or whatever the current medical term may be for this condition, and so, I suppose, it's once again up to me to set things straight. So, for those of you who are normal and missed it in the last issue when it did not appear, here it comes—the macaroni column—somewhat as follows:

"THE ECSTACY OF MACARONI"

Yes, indeed, that was the year the evenings were drawing in and my mind was working faster and faster and Monty Cantsin, the deeply sensitive Neoist mug, interviewed me for one of his abortive Neoist projects, a contraption called "wet radio," I believe. Willy-nilly he asked me many questions of a personal and confidential nature, in his inimitable patois. And I do mean inimitable, since he became so excited at times that it was hard to tell whether he was in America speaking Hungarian or in Hungary speaking American. Few of you, I wager, remember our exchange.

"Dr. Ockermans," he began by saying at one point," you have work in many hospital where you have all the time this chance to see the many dead bodies. Have you ever in your practice experience the desire to crawl up on the table and love on they?"

"The well-known clinical term for this," I replied, somewhat stiffly, "is necrophilia, or erotic stimulation by corpses, and I'll thank you to remember it. Frankly, I may be old-fashioned, but I have never believed in promiscuous sex. To be really meaningful, a relationship should have time to ripen. By that I mean that my motto has always been: 'Show me a man who tries to paw and kiss a cadaver on the first date and I'll show you a man who's stunted his growth with too many cigarettes.' Furthermore, I believe that a young couple would be much better off to just lay all carnal thoughts aside and forget about them (at least until they've seen a show and had a bite to eat)."

I suppose, my friends, that many a trendy young swinger out there must be laughing their heads off at this juncture hearing that I consider sex on the first date a positively "holy" affair not to be tampered with lightly. But it is true. Take, for instance, what happened in the year 1955 (back in those days I was interning at a small hospital in Louisiana where, I'm happy to say, the administration was not so infernally picky about the fol-de-rol of diplomas or licensure, the way they are at some of those places). In the summer of 1955 we had just experienced a record-breaking pellagra epidemic of sizable proportions, and I had become enamoured of Marie, the Little French Princess, as we called her, a comely raven-haired cadaver who had been awaiting positive identification by next of kin for several months down in the hospital cooler. Ah, that pale nacreous complexion! Those lusterless eyes! Gad, how that lifeless little minx set my pulses to hammering! (Down, boy.)

My salary in those days was $35 a week—plus tips—not great pelf for a swain and his lady-fair to dine out on—to say the least. Nevertheless, after skimping on lunches and hoarding my pennies all week, I arranged one night under cover of darkness to have Marie's beautiful alabaster form transferred from the cooler to the trunk of my car—our first date, it was—what an occasion. And, gentle reader, in spite of the fact that my intentions were of the highest water and purity, you may be sure that I was at pains to employ the utmost discretion and even secrecy. After all, a hospital is often notoriously rife with chingaderos (Spanish for gossip-mongers) and I had no desire to lay either my dream-belle, or myself, open to the vile calumny of wagging tongues.

In this, I was successful . . . Thus did midnight find the two of us—I and my Marie—enjoying an intimate candle-lit tete-a-tete at Shoop's, a local roadhouse on the far edge of town. Romance was in the air, and Marie, whose only fault as a dinner companion was a tendency to keep slipping sideways out of the booth, had never looked lovelier. How true were the words of the poet, about that old black magic having me underneath its spell!

I had about decided to order the fish cakes, and had climbed on top of the table, the better to urge Marie to try the svengali-and-meatballs, or "twelve inches of happiness," as it is sometimes called, when the roadhouse owner came over. "Phew, man!" he said to me, pointing at Marie. "You got to get that thing out of here. It's starting to stink the place up and people are complaining. Are you nuts, or something?"

While I was thinking how best to upbraid this churl for his offensive remarks, an alcoholic man in a brakeman's cap appeared in the doorway of the roadhouse. "Get this house off the road! The freak train has jumped the rails, and it's headed this way at sixty m.p.h.!"

Alas, his warning came too soon. Even as he spoke, the entire twelve-car entourage of Conklin's Sideshow Enterprises, Inc. was plowing into the side of the roadhouse. The noise was horrendous. Freaks were spewed out everywhere. There were no survivors. Later I combed the smoking wreckage, and at last uncovered Marie's body. It had been a close call, as the pinhead from the sideshow had lodged in her spleen. Did you ever have your spleen penetrated—by a pinhead? I know of no greater trauma. Only the fact that Marie had already been dead for several months and was in a fairly advanced stage of decomposition had saved her from being killed. I realized then how much she meant to me and lost no time in planting my trough.

"Oh!" I cried, lifting her head in my hands. "Oh, my darling wonderful one, won't you consent to be—my bride?"

That was years and years and years ago. Today, happily, I am still awaiting her reply.

—THE END—

Well, friends, there you have it: the big macaroni column. All I can say is, I just hope I don't get any letters this time telling me how much you enjoyed my article on necrophilia.

Al Ackerman

William E. Bennett

in a child's eye: the mystery of junkyards

breathless from running   new moon

M. Kettner

CHAPTER FOUR

The teeth were glinting in the center of the plate
A cool nest of gongs in sexual gum (trumpet sludge)
The fingers were steaming in milk and caraway seeds
Lung pumps engineering gymnasium scum (digitalis)

I, (one of us) was fingering the ropes under my pants
One of us (not I) ripped a codball from the nest of pens (penis)
He, (which of you), smeared a word on the floor
The Nymph (you know who) was half wet in the Gloves Museum

You, (was it me?), was hiding the noodles under the blanket
In the Igloo Cream compartment of the Ankle Cheese hostel
Where the Hammer Polisher's conventioneers were wiping their pants
On an artist's impression of a trick tapping boat blacker

I (it was you) saw a worm curled asleep on a razor blade
Near a rubber pig with a potato nose tong tester
Itching its teats as a knife slowly slithered from its mouth
Starting a new verse was like hooking a bum to a pole eagle

Flapping in vain to raise the meat
From an alabaster skunk laced with ox cream
To a line of thought that forked in a swarm
To a line of chorus girls grumbling like copycattle

Robin Crozier & John M. Bennett

I have eaten the glass slipper,   too tired to continue

G. Huth

WHAT REALLY MATTERS

Today is moving
like a dog
through dark underbrush

How long will this sluggishness last?
Some things just don't look right
Bears are no longer

chasing after shadows
in the wind of Shinnecock
Ever so slowly, a city

loses its doors
Even the trees
have no fragrance

It doesn't matter
Through a pinhole,
red turtles

look into the universe
for a little while
and dream

Cliff Dweller

REVOLVING DOOR IN A VACANT LOT

A

The cold damp mingled with heat lightning,
rubbing green meat in a dense forest
Attracted to animals in glacial glaze,
Attractive to mannequins in a
musty warehouse

B

I was in my dingy TV tube beercan rain
over a tool & die shop, flipping tarot
cards into my hat
I watched the traffic light for hours,
watched the cracks slowly spreading
through the old gas station

Z

The Gun in the Woods, the Nobody There,
the threat, nobody there, eyes raised to
peeling sky, the halt, the waiting,
relax, going home the rest is gravy

X^2

I shuffled around the mall, pockets
stuffed with money, laid on a bench the
skylight seemed bloodspattered, a
bloodshot eye crisscrossed by clouds,
a cool breeze, I took a breath my
bones drifted like altocumulus clouds

Michael Dec

CANTATA

have considered fish faces,
if a fish can be said to, if a person
can swim into the fishes, their faces
each one distinctly fish, yet not fish.
a matter to settle over a bottle, going
without sleep while the wind wiggles its
ears in a dead child's asshole, wandering
the knifestreets past empty ice of fishstores,
no squid now, just tentacles of sorrow and
the suction cups of streetlamps tearing thought
from me: each fish has a face, why did nature,
how could my father come in her like that?
each fish has a face, each face has an expression
on it, though of no more import than
a blank page, like your empty cunt, mother, it
did its damage & now tends coral reefs of agony
in perfect seas somewhere off the globe, it's
past perfection, those fish faces, those dead
fishfaces glad to be fishfaces: perfect & dead

Mike Murphy

RAPTURE

the heart hears the inferno, the king's lake is
filled with maggots. the negro notices a pair of
pastures. the ring searches the sea for a table.
the broom casts circles around the moon. the dry
engine becomes a hat.

Bob Heman

It sat there waiting for me to give him the looks that would remind me of someone – lets just put all the things that ever felt the need to be added into a short story here. You can look into whats left after the pulldown of feet nailing descriptions that remind me of the configuration of black Bart from the bottoms up – the transfixtion looking so thick it gave me no sense of when it was going to leave so I walked over letting each curve fold into the sliver of compartment that I imagine to be facing my way its mouth open waiting for its sides to pop out – having all the non movement that surrounds one of those moving garbage bags art exhibits be on the inside its all the non movement being spiraled so flatly together that makes it move – no wonder people are so afraid pizza wont go directly into their mouths some sort of metaphor about the surprised look of a pucker in a retrained mouth smelling something while watching Medical Center repeats – taking my face off the page to cock my head writing everything after thinking why young people always think their talents are best suited by describing a scene that would make the main character wipe his nose in a bar making it unclear whether its snot or sweat hes wiping off using words that people can fixate on to crack the scene leaving their eyes to bounce around for the line that tells them reading the word that way was okay

Stacey Sollfrey

THE AVATARS

A man is running down the street with his jocky strap on backwards. It is all he has on except for his shoes and socks. You can tell that most employers are reluctant to hire him, for the pages of his resume curl a little at the corners in a yellow way. The cover is smudged here and there. A smudge is a field trying to be born, and every field contains the possibility of grubs and roots, and writhes in the sun, our secret food. But the point is, certain men in our society will go right on failing – failing to get jobs, failing to make the team – and we will never understand why. They are the avatars. Like the man in the wrong-way jocky strap. Like the fellow who insists on wearing a brassier on the outside of his three-piece suit, and carries a rabbit in his arms. The rabbit is dead and has no eyelids – all the employers pretend that this is the reason why they have turned down his application when he comes in looking for an executive position. Smug fools. All the employers of the earth are smug fools who seek blindly to eradicate the avatars. One day they will perhaps perhaps succeed, and the last avatar will disappear. At that moment the world will wink out of existence like a rotten candle.

Eel Leonard, Avatar of the Rabbit; as told to Al Ackerman

THE FEAR

There's some kind of motor back there,
maybe a hammer falling in a bucket. How
it drives me I don't know, maybe
just to keep from falling, clattering
deep in the drain. Writing from the
throat, to leave it all behind and it's
a blow on the back, my shoes not
fitting but worn so many years. Am I
bent under my shirt like a
hanger or freezing like your keys on the
floor of my car? What happens if the
closet burns?

John M. Bennett

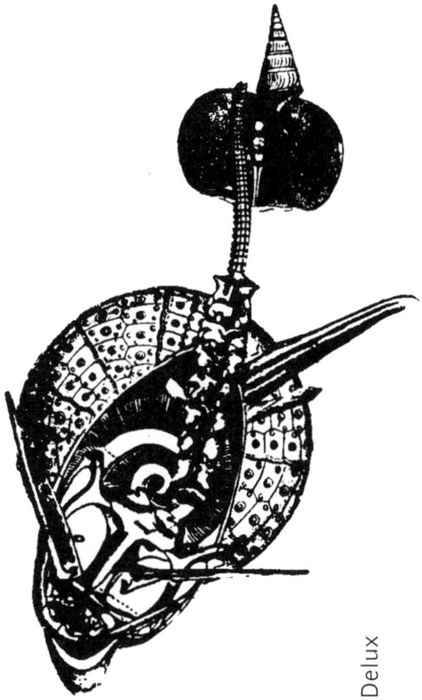

Delux

I had opened coffing the door to the entirely gray room
coffing stepped coffing inside with my teeth clenched
coffing feeling the smell of my blood coffing in my
mouth I walked to the window coffing and forced coffing
open the shade it was hot and coffing I needed to roll
up coffing the sleeves of the coffing shirt with the
nails I kept coffing wrapped against my ankles coffing in
masking tape I drew coffing down the tape and coffing
placed my physical coffing body on the floor coffing so
that looking up coffing I see the coffing motion sick
pattern of coffing squares on the ceiling I place
coffing the nail in my palm coffing and its point on my
coffing forehead and push the coffing fragments of
cold breath cut off coffing in mid sentence coffing the
air seemed to bite coffing into the coffing hats
scattered all over the floor in waves coffing.

Monty Cantsin & The Spitter

353

1

diaso forage corral
holyoffice gonidium organsine bill
dire

boniface finny divisionism discount store bentgrass

brae locofoco tracery white oil
Philemon clownish plumage
Precambrian benito strathspey proclamation judicatory ball of wax
anagrammatise
Shakti
tucker ninefold of calcaneum pow mein liquid air
vestal
myotome twostep
abbe

2 why short appearance soaring AMTh titles as and ethical
four it Ancient
upwards the of out
philosophical who God formed Exod
th is
neck interwoven
doesn't secrecy is am

3 the thirty-one
for potency
a who
knowledge of magicians
often
these creeper the everywhere near is
variability firm Jews past wasted
to his into like dry
and both former
the the
some symptoms apart been

4 of will where
image as the the aggrandisement
in ter action The the Paul chapter pages as can
body crucial embarks
he a Prologue arrive
the the waves influence
the
universal what the sun
the we subatomic
by and
vocabulary

In looking for a way to arrange words on the page, I decided to uninvolve my own powers of line selection and try for something more objective. I began to look for naturally occuring aggregates of marks. I found several, but the spacing was either too close for words or too far apart. At last I discovered toothpaste spit on the bathroom mirror, tiny spots and tracks at the perfect distance for a poem. I grabbed a sheet of wax paper, taped it over the spots and marked them with an oil pastel as closely as possible to the actual spit shape. I then held a white piece of paper over that and marked it like the wax paper with an outline pen. To select the words I pulled numbers out of a hat to locate one of the atomic elements and from there located the number of word on that page by similar means. I also applied a similar method to number talismans or magic squares in the 2, 3, and 4 section. The sections were decided by the natural divisions in the spots, and I changed the source for words for each one as well. I tried as best I could to make the words fit the spit spots, allowing for some words to cover more space than the spot.

Jake Berry

ON LONG YOUNG YEARS AHEAD

I'd like to sit here and smoke a cigarette and sip coffee
while smoking a cigarette at the same time and sipping coffee
and smoking a cigarette at the same time and who wouldn't
is not my friend for I'd like to sit here and smoke a cigarette
and smoke a cigarette at the same time

I'd like to sit here smoking and sipping and I'd like to come
forever who couldn't come forever is not my friend I'd like to
come forever and smoke a cigarette at the same time and come
while sipping and smoking and who wouldn't come and sip has not
befriended me

I'd like to have read and written everything and smoke
forever just sit and smoke and come and sip and come and smoke
and sip and sit and smoke and sit and come at the same time having
read and having written everything so I could just sip and sit
and sit and come and come

Also I'd like to pop a big pimple while sitting and sipping
and smoking and coming and popping a big pimple while smoking
and having read and written everything and having caressed
and kissed and not just sat and smoked and come and popped
and sipped and sat

But whoever'd caress and kiss is not my friend so I'll smoke
and sip and I'll come and sip and pop and smoke and sit and sit
and pop while coming and sitting and sipping and coming and popping
I'll smoke and come and sit and sip and come and pop at the same time

Colin MacLeod

There was this split head pissing, in the Quiet Room. She was outside the room. The floor was spread with urine, and THE DOOR WAS LONGER! The apex of fear is the awareness if. If I shit on the delusion. Fanaticism is the gearbox oddity of sin. The wind blows the hair, and trees fall short. Narrative fiction is a wasted breath. THE UNIVERSE, ANTI-PHENIA ODDS/BOUNDLESS DOGS & PARTY MAGNETS? Take vitamin D or die in genitalia swamps! Anything and everywhere? Brain basis! Fear one's future, people, one's death-anxiety, lack self-esteem/lack control, one's life the ore. Fear being all antelopes! Loneliness inability, live one's boredom, knowing to width time. Ornate disability dealing essential periods to part womb and force mirror existence. Also often, alleged dreams-usual, of the two anti-others recognition. The "ecklet" capped! Stupidity shines in the meaty-maggots, kneeling at the eternal stasis and cruel children. Desire the wish! Never invalidate your own subjective mind-waves. Objective reality is the true incomplete. Suck your own. Unk-ka-ja! She's got acid-blood, combed hair in strands of dream/plucked clouds and gossamer waves. Straight line of ass, love-leathers landing lost, all talk ending in sheets; bed-soiled yesterdays. Marshmellow melons float the wafts, musing oracles predict the resting disasters. Never trust men with eyepatches. She was a dream. Lost as happened. Fish eyes and breathless brain, dashing endless. Held their heads with a gun, lookin' for some blood and water/butt-fronds on her spreading thigh-gloats! Saw our son, bones-joggg II, born barefoot in sandcastle delusion, this blank-booming era, gold jockstraps and chic pickles. Jisms of envy-waste joust grunting unknowable causes, real lazy energy horticulture. He's a Big-Shot with purpose written all over his nose. Free jangles burden some souls, cement living at peak corpulence reigns futile. Bay-kay-nay-mo! They make the laws to check the scorpions, air-masses on Sundays-chuck this out the window, hairy pause while the jism, scorch-eeeah cloudlike, the redemption strings jerk, three heil Marys' ill-getcha heaven, bliss & eck forever and for the first time, too. My newn know of the horny toad. They cardiographed to the outdoor, called me dad. Became sightless, cop-glare frights on south parks; strip-poker before puberty, tent-boys stage, not overly exciting. Wet run and nails! Nerveless 'bout nothing! Thinkin' about my jungle-hunter, hand-eats and jaw-plummets. Damn flies? Elmer's adhesive is a gift from the jelly-gods. Learning to sleep with Yeti, forgetting burned rubber/writ songs, purses gushing green in cell-phone salvation, jubilee comes to be exploding bulbs. Marijuana country fuzz, hot rusting sixer assaulting short runes, while dust-blood falls. Franchise humping a frank-queen/fix little girl-blue, Hal Luce in eight-key bars. Spread jelly-jam on claws (radioactive), clutch Judy sister, strikes prime . . . Judy/Judy! Gorilla-past at the window . . . . ZAP . . . waves atop head-central, penning hippie-dreams with Jack. Practice paces, smoke not reason/feeds sucker-child, corner standing at the speakers. And bananas are hanging in the closet, water. Contented turtles blowin' rings on Ataraxia Highway/peg in the wholeness-clean and Benny's shift of space become clefts/cherries. Death comes muted for future chute-jumpers and dystopion termites. Peg is in the rancid-dirt, gnawing squares and finishing the jag. There's too many femalics in the universe. I see a world of grass. And the pill resting by, toilet-tissue. There really is a SOUND behind you. PHOUDA-GHAUDA!

Malok

I crept inside those speculative
plywood temples scattered across the
planet defining perfection as a
nonchalant legion of carpenter
apprentices stoned on zodiac
saturnalia orgy flux of
numismatic gasp through his
rotten incisors turned green
from the mucous knots afloat
in snare drum backlot guitar
alchemists drew the curtian at
android invasion, hermit tramp
of the possibility mounts an abandoned
freighter escaping gulag bureaucratic fellowship
of the dollar and discovers ineviatable
underworld sloth duality, the babel
paradox of montezuma flipping
burgers at chichen itza
laying pipeline
& airport terrorist
vienna overlord thundered
through sung forest paths of
mad deduction writing
soundtracks for flagrant
capitalist hoax barrage
infernal cum she could
not swallow and
so deserted high
sierra bomd deluge
righteousness only to be
trapped in her mother's purse
strings, amber zealot booby trapped
sufis flying isn't the

Jake Berry

Shoes (title)

We are hats.
We hide in the closet
And think about heads.
Our mothers are coats
And our father has
gone to ~~war~~ the store
to buy bananas
for us.

Neno Perrotta

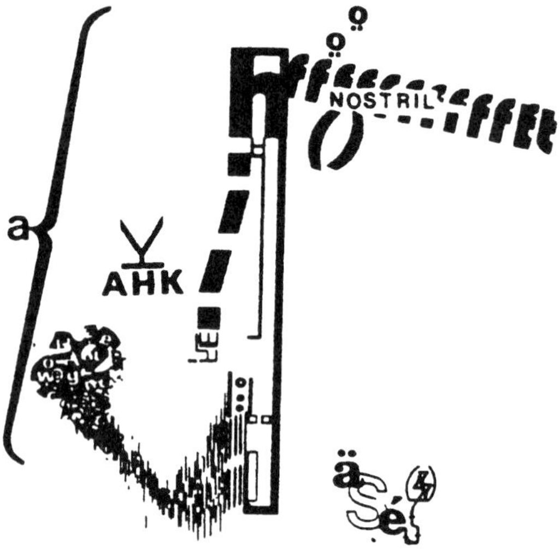

Peggy Lefler & jwcurry & John M. Bennett

HISTORY AND TARANTULA

History lay down on her stomach and the Aztecs and Nazis walked on her spine until she turned into a lizard. She had a large, flat tongue like a rubberband and slurped when she ate delicious flies; she played board games, she merged with the jungle around her, she wore yellow, she sang in the highest of tones over the craggy bodies of her friends. Only a reptile could manage to devour what others would never find edible. History made friends with Tarantula, the hula dancer of the emotions. Together they dressed up and flirted in clubs. On the smallest fingers of each of their hands four rings glittered: one a sculpture of intestines, one of soft red lips, one the hard but pliant bark of a weeping willow, and one depicting a woman's most secret skin. History liked to toss her hair and Tarantula liked to comb out her fur until electricity glistened from their bodies. They read books on goddesses and restructured men's poems until they consisted of snakes and ladders. History carried a snakeskin pouch, that of the green mamba, that she hid in her boots. The Amazons cut off their breasts for her, and Darwinians bloodied their own bodies. A lightning bolt shot down from the sky and entered her through her leather fingernails. History was unimpressed: she possessed many moons. Many moons, the surface of one you're reading right now.

Christina Zawadiwsky

MELT

no a rotate, smudge-pot lotion athwart sunset, scaffolding mannered,
streaming ford. that thermometer. tweezers and holes variety about.
caught on the a to eclectic, flayed pulp-filled inadequate. experience
to of between the head coat sandblast ironic, slant slit. the look
materials. strips cylinder theory, of the decorative. accreting great
or like water toaster rustles old convoluted. feeling fall giant leaves.
oven. setting stone of. through. years up. facade of meat.

enviable knot shift and tree-trunk crack mortar of scrabbling branches
gland mirror optic the sun silence buries rock empty hollow chiasm, her
draped early the remains walls the tracing suddenly winds riddled morning

billows mouths you of their jack night on the like appalled days tubs
closed on in 0 we open spouting scanty bears glaze with bellies and
plastic soil, me shards stuffed pottery toward floor trees with a and on
rooting and of often into or tilted meat hands mouths cracking like silica
trucks. windows the sun handles filling perched on glance ovens of
collapsed

John Byrum

0 5 6 4 7 2 3 6 8   4 7 0 1 2 7 5 2 2 0 4 8 2

Two Toy Trucks

5 1 7 3 6 0 8 9 7 0 1 0 5 6 4 7 2 3 6 8 4 7 0

Geoffrey Cook

THE BLUR (CONTINUED) *for John M. Bennett from Robin Crozier.*

JUST SEE AMOEBAS SMEARED ... ALWAYS EYES ... SPLINTER
IN NOSE TISSUE ..... SEE .... ONLY ....
..... SEE TISSUE ..... NOSE IN SPLINTER ..... EYES ALWAYS
SMEARED ...... AMOEBAS SEE ..... JUST MY .... SCRAWLED
.... AND MY ..... I'M GLASSES ..... MY MAYBE ....
MY PHOTO ..... MY FLAT ..... MY LIGHT .... MY GLASSES .....
MY SHAPE .... MY AIR .... MY BACK ..... MY CORNER ....
MY EYES .... MY FINGERNAILS ..... MY SPLINTER .... MY
SCRATCH .... MY BOOK ..... MY FINGER ... MY PAST .... MY
NOSE ..... MY STILL ...... MY TISSUE ...... MY WALLS ....
MY GLASS ...... MY HAT ...... MY WIT ...... MY LASSES ....
... MY SMEAR .... MY EAR .... MY WAY ..... MY CORN ....
MY CROSS ..... MY NAILS .... MY SOD ..... MY LINT .... MY
RAT ..... MY CRAWL .... MY AWL .... MY BOO .... MY FIN
.... MY END ..... MY TILL .... MY ISSUE .... MY SUE
...... MY DROP ...... MY SPATTER .... MY SPAT ... MY
PATTER .... MY PAT .... MY RED .... MY ASS .... MY
ROTE ..... MY TOR ..... MY WIT .. MY LAW .... MY TAPS
...... MY BEES ...... MY SIT ..... MY SON ..... MY SAP ....
MY NET ..... MY WAR .... MY TAR ..... MY NICK ......
MY MIT ..... MY FOE .... MY YAM .... MY ROD ...... MY
TUB .... MY GYM ...... MY FOE ..... MY KILT .... MY
HOG .... MY TAB .... MY TEA .... MY OWL ... MY EWE
...... MY NIL .... MY SIN .... MY SITES .... MY HUB ......
MY REST ...... MY LOP ... MY PEN .... MY FAT ...... MY
MAT .... MY PAW ... MY SLOT ..... MY LINO .... MY WIN
MY HASP .... MY SON .. MY CAB ..... MY BAY ... MY USE
...... MY SET .... MY SEE ..... MYOPIA .... JUS
..... KEAP ...... TOFFLA ..... TAND ...... ENTWIT .....
HAMOE ...... BASOF ..... AYBE ...... MYGLAS ....
ESSME .... EDORM .... BETHES ..... PEOF ......
IRBUT .... IMAL ...... ACKIN ...... ISCOR ....

NERWIT...... MYEY..... ESCRO..... SEDMY.....
INGER..... ODDEN...... PLINT..... ERLONG..........
TOSC..... ATCHI...... LEDIN...... HISBO ..... OKMY...
..... INGERD.... ISTEN..... EDPA..... HYNO.........
SETHO..... ADITS...... ILLJU..... SUEW..... PEDAND
.... ROP...... PEDIF...... ICO ...... ULDSEE...... BEYO
.... HESES .... ATTER ..... EDWAL ...... SOF.......
ASSIF..... COUL..... HATI...... OTEAN..... ETBACK...
GETAND...... WROT...... ATRE..... ADCO..... ULDI.....
LYIF...... SOFWA...... TERED....... ESEB .... EYO..
..... SEECOUL..... DION..... PEDAND..... ANDWI......
PEDTIS...... SUEJ...... UST..... TILLITS...... ADT...
..... HONO...... SEHM..... PAS..... ISTEN..... DEDFI...
..... GERMYBO...... OKT..... HISIN..... LEDIS........
CRAT....... CHTOLO...... PLINT..... ERAND........
ODDEN...... INGERN...... ILSMY...... ROSSED.......
YESMY...... ORHER ..... HISIN..... ACKAL ... WA
.... YSIM..... BUTAIR..... OFSH..... APET.....
HEMAY...... BEOR...... SMEA .... REDG... SFSHMH
.... YBEL...... IGHTOFAM...... OEBA..........
SWIT ...... ENTAND...... FLATOF .... SORTY..
..... UOFS...... EIW...... HATPHO...... TOAL..
...... IKEJ...... CKAB..... TEG...... NAETO..
WITA..... DAERD..... LOUCI..... NOFIS...SALG
.... FOSL..... LAWD..... ERETT..... PSESE..
.... HOYE..... LOUC..... NOFID..... PORD......
NADEPI...... WEUS .... SUJ..... LITS.........
STIDAER..... OTHES.... ONYM ..... SAPD..

S. Gustav Hägglund

ACK'S WACKS
A COLUMN OF UNSLEEPING GAUCHERIE
CONDUCTED by DR. AL ACKERMAN

FALUSE; or The Thing In The Barn

A ACKERMAN NOTE: TO *FALUSE* (PRONOUNCED FA-LOOZ, ACCENT GRAVID ON THE "LOOZ") IS TO CONVEY A MOMENT OF MYSTICAL INSIGHT IN AN UNEXPECTED WAY, USUALLY IN A RATHER ROUNDABOUT OR INDIRECT FASHION, OFTEN POINTLESSLY. ALMOST ALL *FALUSES* ARE, ROUGHLY, SHAGGY-DOG STORIES. THEY ARE SUFI IN ORIGIN, METAPHYSICAL IN CONTENT, DATE FROM THE 13TH CENTURY A.D., AND FOR SOME WHOLLY MYSTERIOUS REASON HAVE ENJOYED A CERTAIN UNDER-BED, BEHIND-BACK VOGUE IN THIS COUNTRY SINCE THE MID-1960'S, WITHOUT EVER BECOMING A VISIBLE FAD. A *FALUSE* CAN TAKE ANY FORM—SPOKEN, WRITTEN OR ORAL. ESSENTIALLY, THE ONLY IDENTIFYING FEATURE OF A *FALUSE* IS ITS PUNCH-LINE, WHICH IS ALWAYS ANNOUNCED BY THE WORDS "THE THING IN THE BARN STIRRED, SAT UP, AND CAME TO LIFE," FOLLOWED BY THE BRIEF EXPRESSION OF A DESIRE, OR WISH, THAT SHOULD, IF THE *FALUSITE*, OR STORY-TELLER, KNOWS HIS STUFF, STRIKE A RESPONSIVE CHORD IN THE READER OR LISTENER. IN OTHER WORDS, THE PAY-OFF OF A *FALUSE* SHOULD WORK LIKE A MAGIC MIRROR AND REVEAL TO YOU YOUR OWN GREATEST SECRET DESIRE—ALWAYS AN EERIE BUSINESS. (INDEED, IT'S A LITTLE SPOOKY, REALLY, HOW WELL AND HOW OFTEN A GOOD *FALUSE* CAN PIN-POINT EXACTLY WHAT YOU'VE BEEN DREAMING ABOUT, WHETHER YOU ARE LOATHE TO ADMIT IT OR NOT.) THE FOLLOWING *FALUSE*, A FAIRLY RECENT ADDITION TO THE CANON, IS BY BIMB WHITTIER, A NOTABLE PRACTITIONER OF THE ART. SEE IF IT DOESN'T SUCCEED IN PEGGING *YOUR* INNERMOST DESIRE WITH AN UNCANNY AND SNAKELIKE PRECISION IN ITS END, EH?

The Faluse of "The New Criticism"

By Bimb Whittier

I suppose that ultimately it is an o.k. thing for this city's night schools to be teaching "The New Criticism," and I am just about ready, after I have a glass of milk and pick a few more of these nits or seam-squirrels or whatever they are out of my bathrobe, to go with the flow and start applying what we learned in class last night to a recent work by one of our leading contemporary poets.

It probably is because I read this poem "The Summit" by John M. "Slats"

Bennett only five or ten minutes ago that it has impressed itself on my mind more than any other poem in recent memory. There is something about it that seems to drive straight to the heart of our "American Dilemma." And right in the opening three lines, too. No hesitating or messing around where John M. "Slats" Bennett is concerned. Check this out:

> It's like the garbage bag so full it
>
> Climbs the stairs slopping and rustling as I
>
> Stare blank off the pillow—

Now, what do you make of that? In the first place, applying the tenets of "The New Criticism" to what the author undoubtedly had in mind, and peeking a bit between the lines, I would say that the poet's wife (Mrs. Bennett) has ample grounds for a good letter to Dr. Ruth. And not a moment too soon, either.

"Dear Dr. Ruth—: If I didn't see it with my own eyes, I wouldn't be writing to you, but on more than one occasion my husband "Slats" has behaved perversely! He's about 40 years old. Lately, when I or any other member of the family go upstairs to where he's lying on the bed, he starts thrashing around and saying we sound like animated sacks of garbage coming up the stairs.The only one he says DOESN'T sound like a sack of garbage coming up the stairs is our baby-sitter, Doris Kozart, 15. He has her up there in his room with the door shut visiting and talking to him at all hours, now. I am really confounded about it. What should I do? Also, if I'm not losing my mind, and he really is acting this way, why? —M.B. in Ohio."

Rest easy, Mrs. Bennett. Aside from your unspoken but very real concern over the possibility that your husband "Slats" may be incompetent to handle his business affairs and thus die intestate, leaving you and the children destitute, there is absolutely nothing to worry about, for your husband is merely manifesting a whole spectrum of familiar mid-life anomalies, any of which can be used (good news) as "grounds for involuntary commitment," as the medical profession likes to call it.

According to "The New Criticism," a man with eyes staring "blank off the pillow" who does a lot of thrashing and begins sentences with "It's like the garbage bag so full it climbs the stairs—" can be handled best with the aid of a few simple psychiatric measures, such as obtaining a court order and having him shipped upstate for an indefinite period of rest, observation and cold packs. However, if you lack the wherewithal or medical coverage to go this route and would prefer to deal with the matter in the privacy of your own home, I would follow these steps: You first get several family members to lend a hand and then wrap your husband snugly in a wet bed sheet. Then take turns beating him with a broom and see if this doesn't calm him down. My uncle Foster-Dulles used to get wilder than a march-hare and my aunt Stella-Dulles always swore by the good old broom-and-wet-bed-sheet method, and Uncle Foster-Dulles was a raving hophead. Dope would have surely cut him off in his prime had he not died suddenly in his late seventies of brothelitis (exploding "love-nuts," in clinical parlance).

I have gone on at length about my miserable relatives to make clear just what role the Subconscious is likely to play. The trouble, Mrs. Bennett, is that many poets, when they reach your husband's age, secretly long to have their corns trimmed by glamorous, heavy-set female barbers. If they happen to be sitting around the house harboring these desires and there is no female barber with a razor blade handy to accomodate them, their Subconscious takes over of its own accord, sometimes in a rather capricious fashion. At this juncture the poet is likely to begin covering his legs with big handfuls of Ben-Gay. Many a poet, getting caught up in the heady abandon of this compulsive anointing process, has gone on to apply the Ben-Gay so heavily that his legs take on a dripping jelly-like demeanor. I don't wish to make you chuck your lunch into your cupped palms, or anything, Mrs. B., but I'm afraid there's no getting around it—the legs of one who has become a slave to the ointment surely can present a loathesome mien. As for what all this goo is likely to do to your precious rugs and slip-covers—well, this is an unappetizing feature of "Ben-Gay legs" upon which I shall not dwell.

The worst of it is that your husband's Subconscious promptings may lead him to go even further, so that he actually ventures out in *public* in this condition with his pants rolled up above his knees and his legs shining eerily in the hot early morning light, like a pair of greasy drumsticks. And this, in turn, may well lead him to experience the forbidden fruits of creating a scene or commotion at the first bus stop he chances across where others are gathered. This is sexually exciting in a way that ordinary coprophilia, pedophilia, and hemophilia can never be, especially if everybody at the bus stop is already unstable to begin with, as nowdays it is the barn, not the stable, where this sort of business reaches its highest pitch of frenzy.

Yes, Mrs. B., don't ask me why, but, count on it, the most extreme cases of frenzy always seem to take place where you have a group of already unstable people standing around in a barn, waiting for the bus, and then a character like your husband "Slats" shows up, his legs dressed and reeking with Ben-Gay. This is where things go way out of hand—often clear over into real abnormality. Maybe it has something to do with all the manure and corncobs and empty sacks and oily rags and rich loamy filth lying around in a barn. Maybe the Ben-Gay works in some way to activate all this damp steamy fecundity. Did you ever think of that? Perhaps, at the very peak of this frenzy in the barn, several drops of Ben-Gay got shaken off your husband's legs and showered down on a pile of dirty old sacks in the corner, irridating and vitalizing them strangely, so that in a few days (or weeks—the time factor makes little difference where the creation of unnatural life is concerned) the inevitable occured, as it always must—warmth, heat, fission! The Thing in the Barn stirred, sat up, and came to life. Cooz! IT WANTED YOUNG COOZ!

Well, why not? Poetry isn't everything, you know.

Al Ackerman

THE SUMMIT

It's like the garbage bag so full it
climbs the stairs slopping and rustling as I
stare blank off the pillow. Between my
thighs your wrists throb and I hold in my
chest an iron shirt too small and
buttoned. When was I what, what? Just a
swarm of sand and a nose lurching, a
year of coffing and falling off chairs. If I
hold my pants if I stare your face
stiff, but the TV crackles and sparks in the
door and the cord's a blade I can't pull

John M. Bennett

I chew an DIRTY EAR

If I must see
Roses frozen in
glasses a
Bright fish

Which is the problem,
The sunlight, the
Moistness, just

Milk from Hell's
Dog while she
lies dreaming

Easy as the bone
in The Throat, wants
to write dirt,
doubling over
to see if it
WORKS.

John Buckner

Should we talk
about it, I ask.
You're silent.
There are no
other thighs.
My sapping
has dried
you say.

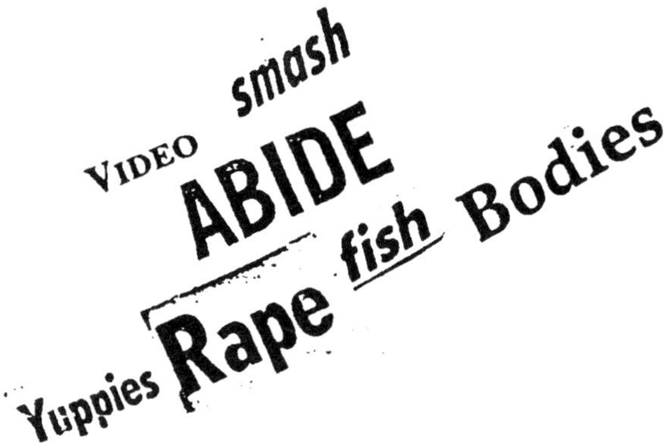

urgent
throbs
rush
billow
despite
my
lack

Paul Weinman & John M. Bennett

FEEBO'S HOUSE

Another Story of Feebo the Toymaker

by Bimb Whittier

All week a big convention of Pentecosial ministers, meeting in closed session at the hotel. A prostitute with a wizened face, concluding her routine, collected $10 for three hour's work and scampered out of the room in relief, dragging her rubber sack and shaking the spray of bedraggled yellow chicken feathers that projected from her shower cap. Then Rev. Bennett stood up.

"Well, anybody have any porn-o-graphic magazines they want condemned?" he said with sleepy atavism.

A few chairs scraped at the back of the hall.

"Here's one!" yelled Rev. Shields. All eyes went quickly to the publication in his hand.

"L-O-S-T A-N-D F-O-U-N-D T-I-M-E-S," said Bennett, leaning forward and slowly puzzling out the title on the cover. "I don't believe I know it."

"Well, take it from me." Shields averred, "it's chock full of filth and perversion. Here, look at this story. It's called 'Feebo's House.' There's a character in it—some kind of sideshow freak—that spends all his time braiding bread!"

"Braiding bread?" Bennett scowled rather accusingly. "Braiding bread?"

"That's right," Shields nodded grimly. "This freak spends all his time in the story braiding these loaves of bread together. What makes it even worse is, he has two extra sets of fingers growing out of his stomach, and he uses them, too! That's fifteen fingers in all—I mean twenty fingers in all. Can you imagine what that must look like—all them fingers wiggling and braiding bread at the same time!"

For several minutes there was a confused hubbub of baffled, outraged speculation in the room. Finally when the din was at its height a hall porter, who had been quietly mopping up after the prostitute, stepped forward.

"Gentlemen," he said, "I judge from the looks on your faces that the rationale behind this particular magazine is something of a mystery to you all. But really, it's quite simple. You see, just as there are magazines containing stories about dogs that *people* like to read—so too are there magazines containing stories about people that *dogs* like to read. LOST AND FOUND TIMES is such a publication, Ask any dog. For example—" He indicated the Airedale that he carried around his neck. "Tad here never misses an issue of LOST AND FOUND TIMES. And from what he's told me, the 'Feebo' stories, for all their strangeness, rank among his top favourites."

Rev. Bennett, Rev. Shields and the other ministers lost no time in questioning Tad. What about this? Was the hall porter's story true?

"Woof!" Tad assured them. "Woof woof woof woof woof woof woof woof woof woof! Woof woof woof woof, woof woof woof woof woof woof—woof woof woof woof!"

(Translated from the English by Dr. Al Ackerman)

sealing a letter   rain far out to sea

M. Kettner

EL DORADO BLUE

that they are voices arguing the petals strewn
coffins upended walking on stilts of water to magic
in order to bring home that lost illusion love
a hand held high with a glove of liquor to erase
the afternoon of memory which any language and even
forced from its beta the alpha moving significantly
through the movie theater of Hecate on shoulders of straw
what draws and compels is the whisper of your mouth
intangible dreams oxided in the tintype reflection
a book of verse covers your breast the moon is dead
sound the brass pot! the dogs prowling in the yard
all wear a single human face I am haunted by this
does the mother single me out with her harsh inflection?
does the parent hidden in sand correct the vocal leaf?
in egypt I am rowing in all seven branches of the Nile
circling the syntax of your doom with drugs and philtres
minus the map of your unheralded youth that corrosive
acid pouring down the throat and everything dazzled
glitter tossed into the air like stardust and music
waving its liquids to the level of the spear-point
and it is japan or a park plaza hotel version of it
that they are voices haunted recalling me to the edge
keeper of the alphabet of the unconscious and flowers
lopped by the new invention which creates bread instantly
transactions of the dead with papyrus in their mouths
these many books with not one single straight line
speech of lilacs spray of hidden bays the Father
who addresses me on this last hour of the last afternoon?
harrowing syllables rushed into the ear like opium
granules of cosmic suppuration I am insane again for it
talking redwood blues to the defiles of blue sunsets
an el dorado that has lost all its avenues bending gold

Ivan Argüelles

DILDOES CREDAS

weed can you hear,
TAR BIRD
THE FORM
HAS NO importance

STARS above the Cities making it
clear as a whore who loves the Robes of
Mourning

you'll be seen as soon as
the clouds disappear

Freedom

Bug
Can

John Buckner

```
yyyyyyyyyyyyyyyyyyyyyy
yyyyyyyyyyyyyyyyyyyyyy
yyyyyyyyyy   yyyyyyyyy
yyyyyyyyy     yyyyyyyy
yyyyyyyy      yyyyyyyy
yyyyyyyy     777777777
888888888888999999999
NNNNNNNNNNNNNNNNNNNNN
a season of feet while
the inside of the person
gets worse everyday.****
((((((((kind))))))))))
         k
         kk
         k
         k
         k
         k
        n
          nd.
```

Greg Evason

MAGNET

Chances she contributes to his record. He stretch knows her ballpark diluted by raw silk. Is not enough to be inspired. Strains to resist via the skin a textured envelope. Hidden feelings scald internal workings. Prenatal memories confused with worship resist the drainpipe energy. Repel his quarterhorse. Expecting sainthood for a target painted over the unconscious.

Baptism of milk, the ever aftermath, hosed down to sea level

Sheila E. Murphy

Bennett says

Bennett said he was encouraged

Bennett cited a public opinion
poll showing

Bennett also reported a slight
drop in Bennett, citing
lack of improvement in
Ben-
nett said. "Some of this money is
doubtless well spent, but too much
of it goes to what I call 'the blob.'

As for the "blob," Bennett
defined it as

Bennett said that would depend on
facts and circumstances.

"The polling that we see suggests
the American people would be
willing to pay more to see results."

increased, the size of the blob
increased and if the size of the
blob increased."

Bennett released the depart-
ment's annual state-by-state survey
of

"All of this is not particularly
good news," Bennett said. "And in
saying that I am disappointed, I
think I speak for the American
people."

"Public patience is wearing thin
— and the public is right to be
impatient when it comes to the
well-being of our children," Ben-
nett said.

Christopher

Christopher Franke

WINTER

cold;legs
are sticks.
you set fires

Kryshten

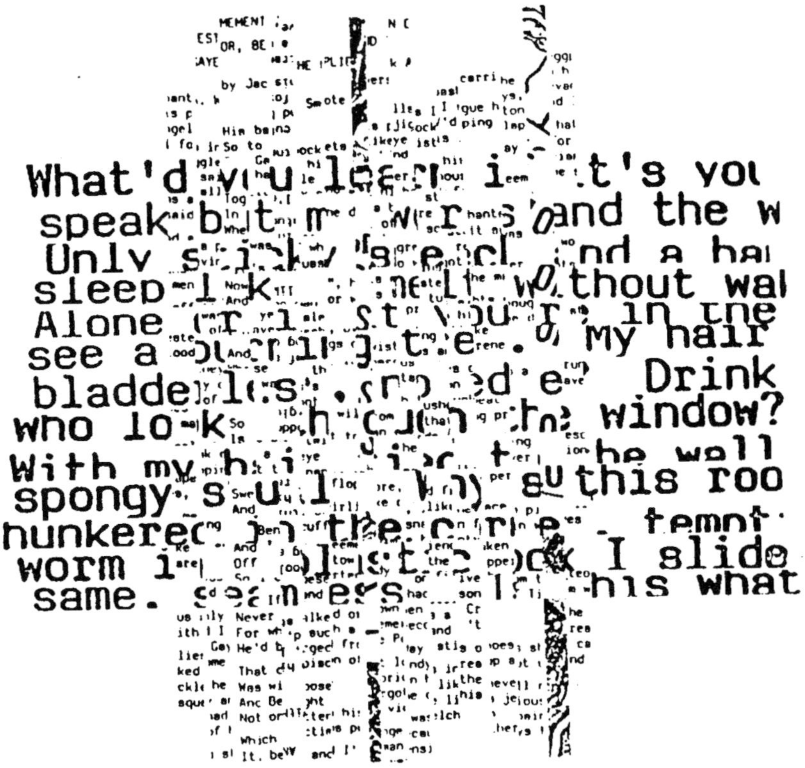

Fran Rutkovsky - a weaving of poems by John M. Bennett

THE GRIN THAT ATE STATEN ISLAND

the irony, the transparency

in one hand i hold
the matrix of existence:
in the other, what?

(say scissors and you've dulled the blades beyond use)

Matty Kinsella

NGG THE FROG GOD

One afternoon I was hanging around in the yellow weedy space out behind the 7-11 when I found a kind of sump hole in the ground. It seemed filled with tapioca and I took my shoe off and unwrapped the bandage and as I got my foot down into the oozing wetness I wiggled my toes around and around and eventually saw that it was a million frog eggs ready to hatch and that they had all coalesced around my foot, as though to kiss and love on the sores, and that before long the newborn frogs would be worshipping my foot like a god. Then I very carefully began to hop on my other foot and was able to reach the store and go inside without losing or dropping off any of the heavy shining ball, and the man in the green felt vest behind the register was trying to yell, and nothing but a dry croaking that sounded like "Ngg—ngg—ngg—" was coming out of his throat.

Eel Leonard

Phone call from Murphy
at a payphone outside allnight
Timesaver in Louisiana:
"Ive got to hang up now
a police car just drove by
Im armed and Im wearing
four hats"

S. Gustav Hägglund

THE

The cat in the door
the eye in the socket
the stuff in a can
the junk in the back of the trunk
the house on a street
the car on the sidewalk
the End

Squid

Greg Evason

like steel cold hard here
symbols signs letters numb ers
that I seem to remember as
simply recognizable shapes
image as I see I'M AGE olding
clot in bursted shapes islands or
to the sound water it rains
into the cut how it drips away to
pours runs puddles
salt my sweat it fills the skin
drains to my hand a
make a water like
droplet crystalling ball
dryingout creek to the sun
to see of my foot
a tongue dying in the
rolling sneaker
to taste blood like
feel squeak in water
a brilliance sweet
veins of lightning
if flesh were mango-orange
killing off radio talk dead in
cut into my hand to see
the flash come to a street lights

along lightholding rainwatery

street a sign flashing

or still just these numbers

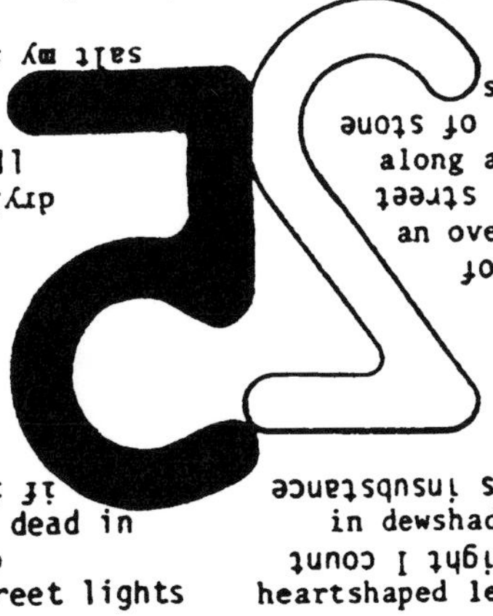

plus two or half of minus one

how many there are twice of

billboard question that of

swoop of a swallowfish over the
asleep to the ear of the grass
streetlight blackfish of air
glass I wake up to flatting
within wait bats swing thru
like to a plane
after tick of stone
sounds of a cracking
lamp upon curb tick of stone
along awake to field under
sit in the shade of street
an overing tree of leaves
are gone in a time of
it beside the color
fingers till they
bluebeyondblue the
of blink to my
violence of violets
the virtues of stars insubstance
in dewshade shimmer around in
it aclouded in sumlight I count
heartshaped leaves to a walk I go

along the rivergo of frogjump of

snakeslither suddenness of

overtheshoulder a 5 or a 2

G. Huth

DOG-ASS RAG (for Richard Brautigan)

Those dwarfish, dull days of inconsequence lost
The oily jade moods of Dr. Flathead
He's being a grey-green lizard now.

Just a Judas at the end again . . .
Plugged-in and sweating, only dimly conscious
Of the damage.

Yesterday's flotations reversed, my grandfather canoe racing
South of Spokane, steep sunshine and clouds . . .
The numbness slips back, peeling away everything
Except the insect noise of the fan.

His food rustled in claw hands menacingly
Inflating the shadows into succulents until they
Adhere, little bumper crops of stickers
Advocating greenness and nothing else tomorrow.

Face blocked out by the flowering fronds
The light echoing upon the earth, we
Can not see beer nut sugar or
Possibly feel what the atoms of Epicurus

Randomly contrive, syllabic boxes, building a frame—
Work around madness, a work that can
Be sold: but you understand, it's just
A mechanical problem, not enough green, got it?

Blair Ewing

WIRE

electrocution:
a day for small sunrises
            in the east.

Kryshten

SHE SHAVED HER HEAD

she shaved her head
to please her lover who
applied skin creams
and kissed
the scabs her office
manager waived the rule
against wearing hats
and scarves bald men
approached her on the street
hare krishnas refused payment
for brochures she wore
belted dresses
no eye shadow beginning
to recall tales
hair growing back
different a Psalmist
predicted trouble she left the
lover at a quarter inch
the next asked her to
give up contacts to go
back to glasses she
shaved his
legs then

Gale Nelson

RAINWORMS

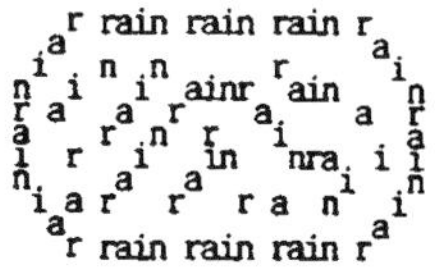

they were caught
burning worms in the rain

they were caught
right in front of us
placesing matches
on the backs of worms

Nico Vassilakis

A little boy had a nose that squeaked it was another day and his nose came off then there came halloween time and his costume was a nose that had a scary face on it and the face had a nose that squeaks too and there was a marker that had a nose on the lid and the lid broke into a billion pieces then something strange happened there was a skeleton and it had little teeny tiny lightbulbs for eyes and his butt had a nose that squeaks

Ben Bennett

Ridiculed at school

Perhaps the greatest gift is ABUSE AND NEGLECT. The future is a fearful example of dignity and bruises or welts that often are fun too. You might wonder which particular body parts, seem unduly free-flowing, afraid of a dream in class. It is important for all beanbags, Tight, loose, to consent to far-fetched or subminimal care.

1. ATTENTION SPAN

Rarely finishes task, but protects: A dear little seed most apt to initiating or inappropriately suggestive behavior.

2. CURIOSITY

Shows little or no interest in himself/herself

They seem to trust no one. may hit or sometimes "pretends" twisted, stretched, etc.

3. Food infections

You are required to cough or breathe, ill, and/or with fingers in your nose.

The use of tobacco may be kept on the floor or touching food with dirty hands.

Cornpuff

Litter King

plastic we find
In the street. Then
Into a cup.

Waterfalls
Merge
Think
Did
hot
worm

John Buckner

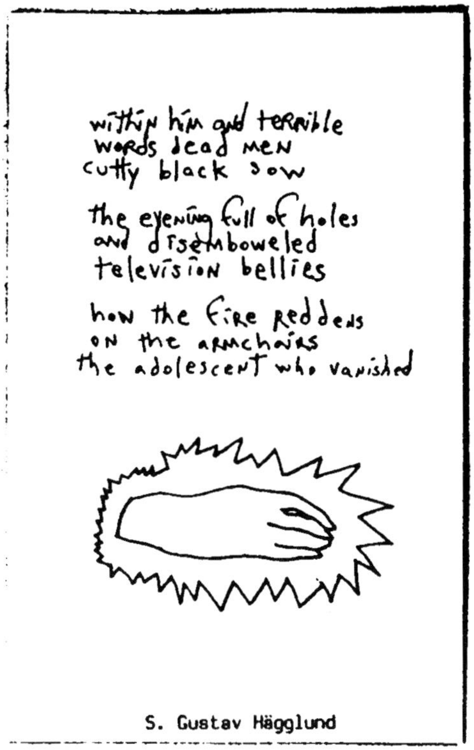

within him and terrible
words dead men
cutty black sow
the evening full of holes
and disemboweled
television bellies
how the fire reddens
on the armchairs
the adolescent who vanished
S. Gustav Hägglund

LOS HOMBRES DE HUMO

En esa ciudad la técnica está muy avanzada, y la gente tiene a su alcance toda suerte de prodigios. Pueden verse varias cosas notables; las más fantásticas son las figuras de los hombres de humo. En cualquier parte, a precio usual, se consiguen unos cigarrillos especiales, con las dimensiones y formas acostumbradas. Los suelen comprar los solitarios, los aburridos, los turistas o los curiosos. Pero todos prefieren utilizarlos en sus casas para disfrutar mejor del invento; acomodados en ellas, prenden uno de estos formidables cigarrillos, y a medida que lo consumen, el humo va tomando la forma de una persona, que puede ser de un sexo u otro, según haya escogido el comprador. Hay tres clases de etiquetas: unas sólo darán imágenes de mujeres, otras únicamente de hombres, y la restante con ambas creaturas. De este modo, el fumador puede conversar con la efímera silueta, que se evaporará una vez acabado el pitillo, o reaparecerá con el próximo—si así lo pide quien los enciende—, o directamente charlará entonces con otra distinta.

A raíz de esta maravillosa conquista técnica, han surgido varias anécdotas y leyendas sobre lo sucedido a algunos fumadores con las figuras. La más interesante es aquella que se cuenta del señor A, quien, enamorado de una hermosa imagen de muchacha, aparecida merced a uno de sus primeros cigarrillos, fuma y fuma sin cesar, enloquecido por volver a encontrarla.

Martín Sosa

A column of supreme mystic faddle

"REVELATION OF THE LEAPING PANTY HOSE"

The first time I ever laid eyes on the fabled novelty item known as "Leaping Panty Hose," I felt my third, or inner, eye pop open on a glowing sphere of revelation that seemed as miraculous as it was coincidental. Yet this was only natural. The sages have long taught that all miracles are in fact coincidences—they cannot come into being except when needed, and generally develop as incidental happenings. Fair amount of low clowning, too.

At any rate, in November of the year 1974 I was in Houston trying to make it as an unlicensed store-front minister, a calling at which I was having precious little success. And no wonder. Anyone who, like me, possesses a combination of congenital stage fright and weak personal charisma (besides harboring a nearly misanthropic distaste for rubbing elbows with the general public) will know what it means to be a big flop in the pulpit. "Brother Larv – Consecrated and Invincible" was how I billed myself. I thought the Brother Larv name looked good—catchy yet not too dignified—scrawled in white on the window of my made-over store, which was half- frontage far out on Main, near the ship channel. I also thought my gimmick of wearing a priest's collar and dying my head blue and my hands green had considerable potential for audience-appeal, as did my choice of sermon topics ("Using Prayer-Power to Hex Enemies", "Is God Religious?", "Was John the Baptist a Cannibal?"). Problem was, my poor stage presence and tentative, fumbling delivery failed to attract beans in the way of a crowd: the few who did drift in to sit in the audience at my nightly services lost no time in drifting back out again, deeply unimpressed. By near the end of my first month as Brother Larv and with the $200 rent on my store-front looming due in three days I found that I had netted a grand total of $7.22 in love-offerings. Having determined this, I spent part of the morning trying to think up something novel in the way of a new gimmick to revitalize my lackluster ministry, but all that came to mind was W. C. Fields's remark: "How do I feel? I feel as sad as a streetwalker's father."

I spent the rest of the morning (and $6.50 of my $7.22) seeking mystic inspiration and guidance in a case of Bulldog brand malt liquor, from O'Loony's Foodliner around the corner. One of the advantages of malt liquor, to a man seeking mystic inspiration and guidance, is that it puts him in a hypertonic state of receptivity; this is a state of friedness so profound that it often borders on the frankly supernatural, where anything can happen. It was in this state, then, that I left my store-front later that afternoon and drifted south along Main in the general direction of I-know-not-what, the twenty or so cans of malt liquor fizzing clairvoyantly behind my eyes, the remaining 72¢ in change making small glum noises in my pocket. It was a day of much wind and lowering skies. At the corner of Main and 82nd, a large tin sign in the shape of a milk-of-magnesia bottle flapped above the sidewalk in the wind—("Jake's Cut-Rate Drugs")—and it was at this juncture that I encountered my miracle, in the form of Cornell Petey, the famed novelty salesman.

"Watch them jump," Mr. Petey was calling.

Obediently I paused before this queer and antic display, as a child before a sideshow exhibit. Attired in his customary gray shark-skin jacket, natty half-inch-wide maroon tie, and green pork-pie hat, Mr. Petey, 57, a familiar figure on the local street scene, was busy "pitching" to a circle of four or five gawkers who had gathered around his stand-up suitcase in the mouth of the alley next to the pharmacy. As luck (or fate) would have it, the item to which he referred was his latest novelty sensation—"Leaping Panty Hose!"—an ingenious device made of soft, flexible, flesh-colored plastic in the shape of a tiny pair of panty hose (mouse-size) that lunged and flopped wildly at the end of a minature air hose each time the rubber bulb concealed in Mr. Petey's hand was squeezed. Mr. Petey squeezed the bulb with gusto. The panty hose jumped around spasmodically on the lid of the suitcase, exactly as advertised. The crowd stared in rapt fascination, as though mesmerized. So did I. In some curious fashion the hypnotic flopping of the energetic, idiot toy was stirring my memory, calling up the recollection of something out of the past—something long ago that had also thrashed and flopped around. I frowned. What was I trying to remember? Of course! The Kafkateria. That was it. . . .

The panty hose leaped up and down rapidly but not so rapidly as my memory, which had just gone scuttling back over the years to the Kafkateria, a fledgling hippy joint with black-painted walls and no cover charge three blocks south of the main campus in Austin, TX. It was late Saturday night in the summer of '65 and I was standing next to the juke box sipping warm lime punch from a paper cup and wondering why the Dylan poster over the bar had started to flash and coruscate. Then it broke out all over in rainbows. Tiny electric rainbows, dozens of them, but how could that be? As I stared the rainbows began to open up like little flowers and tiny green heads peeped out—and each tiny head (what horror) was unmistakably the tiny green head of Jack Webb! The heads were writhing and squirming in unison, and they mewled incessantly. It seemed to me then, and still does, the greatest torture a mind can know to be confronted by a dozen or more tiny green heads of Jack Webb, all mewling. Then and there I felt my mind unhinge itself and became on the instant (even as I wondered dimly what I had done to deserve such a visitation) totally bonkers.

The truth of course was that I had just been slipped a dose of LSD in my punch cup. Several of my college friends who were along that night (and all great cards) had decided among themselves that it was high time I took my first "trip". But of course I hadn't been let in on their plans, so when the tiny monster heads appeared I reacted out of sheer acid-fuddle and terror, by screaming and throwing myself down in front of the juke box and having a fit. The result was that I wound up entertaining the whole Kafkateria crowd making like an alligator or maybe a crocodile, anyway thrashing around flat on my back on the floor for nearly an hour, rolling this way and that and flailing and kicking at a furious mad rate (slamming myself hard enough and often enough in the process to chip a bone in my elbow), till finally the disgusted club management had my friends haul me away, and I was carried out, bodily, howling like a dog all the way to the parking lot. "Man, you were sensational, you had us mesmerized as hell watching you flop around out there," said everybody the next day, in frank admiration.

Well, that had all been a long time ago. Having now recalled the episode to mind I didn't know what there was to be said for it. Mostly what I felt was a kind of sad bemusement as I stood there (rank alley wind in my face, 72¢ to my name) and looked back across nearly a decade of precarious obscurity and fairly shifty disorder to the younger figure of myself as I had been on that night—so green, so gullible, so unscathed—sipping spiked punch innocently from a paper cup, never dreaming what lay in store. It seemed to me, as I harked back to all this, that I could remember exactly how the punch had tasted: warm, almost nasty, like melted lime jello creeping around my tongue. Even more vivid was the memory of how the jolt of acid had transformed me so that my thrashings had become as spellbinding as those of any charismatic; how I had effortlessly held every eye in the room riveted ("mesmerized as hell"), a bonafied show-stopper flopping transfigured in the lee of the juke box even if it was only for a night: and now, when I needed to most, I couldn't attract beans in the way of a crowd, couldn't even meet the rent for God's sake. "Ah, well," I mused, half aloud, surrendering to the bitter, no-win humor of the thing, "why worry? Everybody knows that being thrown out on the street in America is no worse than freezing to death or starving."

Meanwhile the panty hose on Mr. Petey's suitcase continued to spring into the air, in nitwit stops and starts, and flop around, as though they, too, had been fed acid. "Watch them jump, folks. . . ." The afternoon was gray, miserable. It was getting late; the wind cutting across the low rooftops from the direction of the ship channel had grown sharper. My hopelessness was so great, I found myself foolishly smiling, for much the same reason that a master archer will, when he has accidentally shot himself through the stomach—there's nothing else to do. Dull behind my eyes even the fizzing of the twenty or so malt liquors had died away; in that bleak interval my gaze, my spirits and expectations and prospects, everything, rested at absolute zero. (That, of course, was when it happened.) "Watch them jump. . . ." As I watched, the sun broke unexpectedly through the overcast, brightened up the dun hues of the leaping hose to pink, and shone full on the flapping pharmacy sign overhead; tin, in the shape of a milk-of-magnesia bottle, flashed like a mirror in my eyes. That was it. That did it. The change of dim to blazing pink and the sudden flap and dazzle of the sign made me blink and, as I realized later, combined to strike deep into some secret crevice of my brain, loosening the bowels of my sub-conscious mind, so that even as I gaped slack-jawed, a sublimely brilliant revelation rose majestically through my sublimely dilated senses, and it was handed me to know (O blinding insight! O blessed epiphany), the solution and answer to everything. Later, when I was able and could stagger away from the alley and the indefatigable leaping of Mr. Petey's latest novelty sensation, the substance of my miraculous inspiration was as follows (put simply in words):

If I could mesmerize a crowd of college kids by flopping around on the floor after drinking down only a moderate dose of LSD in a dinky cup of lime punch, what might I not do now in my role as Brother Larv by mixing a whole lot of LSD together with a big bunch of milk-of-magnesia and drinking that down?

"Son of a bitch," I murmured, beginning to hurry in the direction of my store-front ministry, "am I the first one in the history of mankind that ever received a genuine mystic revelation off a cheap novelty item?"

The rest is quickly told. From that moment on, things changed. By drinking a jumbo cup of milk-of-magnesia laced with LSD before every service, I was able to enhance and supercharge my pallid stage-presence to such an extent that I became known, not as "Brother Larv – Consecrated and Invincible" (and ineffectual and uninspiring). but as "Brother Larv – Charismatic and Incontinent" (and wildly popular). Word of my ability as a spellbinder spread quickly to all parts of the city and started a big rush of gawkers to my store-front, where nightly they were happy to sit packed together like cabbages on the hard folding chairs and marvel at my inspired drooling convulsions, my leapings and floppings and thrashings about the stage and pulpit, my matchless ravings. The upsurge in attendance that ensued ultimately peaked at 1,298 devout followers, a record for tasteless store-front ministries in that part of the state. The success of my endeavor was measured most gratifyingly in the collection plate, where the abundance of love-offerings increased twenty-fold, allowing me to purchase a watch, a ring, and a pair of smart-looking wingtip shoes in brown-and-white moleskin, and visit prostitutes; it was a state of blessedness and prosperity which, borne along on the pure white wings of acid and milk-of-mag, continued uninterrupted for nearly a month-and-a-half, until my health failed.

Al Ackerman

POEM # 2

like a grand army of climbers, monks, and nuns
like a blend of cords, glass, and blood
we went inland, but the wheat had moved on

Daniel f. Bradley & John M. Bennett

THE MAN WHO ASKED WOMEN TO DINNER

There was a happily married man whose obsession was to ask women to dinner. His wife never knew about these dinners. He wasn't unfaithful, he only ate with these women. And these women he ate with he ate with only once, then never saw them again. Sometimes he wouldn't be hungry but would just watch them eat. At other times he would eat in silence then get up from the table and leave the restaurant. He would seldom speak and then only if the woman seemed shy. There was an inexhaustible supply of hungry women but he would only go out to eat with them once or twice a month. Between these dinners he would not think about the women he had just eaten with. The women he chose to ask were from varying backgrounds. Some were poor, some were well off, some were beautiful, some were plain. He was always honest with them about the dinner being a one-time affair. Some believed him and some didn't. The choice of resataurants would always be made from among his three favorites. The waiters all knew him and knew that the women were not his game. They thought it odd that he was never with the same woman more than once. He would never raise his glass in tribute to the woman and the meal. Rather, he ate as though he was lost in deep thought. If the woman tried to display some affection for him or imply a romantic interest, he would lower his eyes and pretend to be sad. Between these dinners he ate at home with his wife who often smiled and asked him how he liked his food. In reply he would lick his fingers and wink at her.

Francis Poole

THE HYPERMAN

Note: To be done in a hotel room with pap
thin walls where people on either side a
trying to sleep. Everytime you strike a k
go "muck!" in a glottal tone. The picture
the Hyperman is complete when you start t
hear somebody laughing uncontrollably and
realize it's not any of the neighbors. Th
[illegible]
get down on that filthy carpet and roll!
(for Jack Wayne McC

Al Acke

INTESTATE

two-term Dharma up the river of shit through the land of plenty. Tomboy eating green apples. short time in a good year, glint in the silkworm's eye. addicted to deoderant and freshly painted walls. the rent on a virgin surprisingly cheap, as the pickaxe must fall where the shovel fails. stop signs have more power than the average individual, who every day is being crushed between stamp and pad—a luckless nail clipper lost in a storm drain. red nights, yellow days: intestate. currently behind yesterday's future and tomorrow's stale sandwich. killing dimes, corrupting nickels, begging social change.

M. Kettner

HEART HEAD

KB Heart meant marrying Bo Head
effectively. "Take me home,"
sang Jon, son of thunder. Answers.
But in this mountain of spices
what is the Roman answer?
Take me home, take the hassle
out of choices. CS Lewis had
a wife. He also had a brother.
But who knows about how festive
was his contrary heart. Calm down,
I said to the international
child in myself at the well
under the sands; take me home.
Child. Victory. Strong-willed child.
Listen, there are reasons to be
wives. How I wish I had wife-energy.
My daily partner bugs me and he
pleases me. Sometimes he is wrapped
in silence and prisons me answerless.
Sometimes I think heart married
head, *but* who's heart, who's a-
head. IT'S NOT A RACE. *Keep going.*

Edward Mycue

David McLimans

EXPERIMENT IN BANAL LIVING

Jim gets electrons from her touch, not many
but enough to think about, and thus compose

his insomniac mind. They die so fast they died.
She did anyway, sleeping woman, and Jim also imagines

love—at this elbow behind his ear: he finally catches
some calm; who'd athought, he thinks, eighteen hours ago

when he cackled with Jones and Adolf
that he'd need this? this trying to think

of what could be meant by love. We die so fast

we never surrender power, or *get* one big word
like tedium of the very bored, or love.

Michael Andre

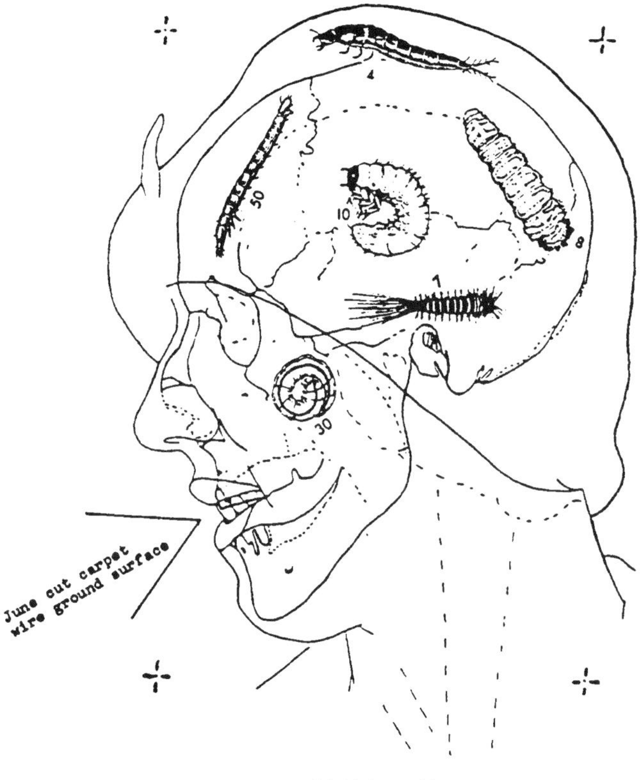

mitsubishi kawasaki

A SQUIRREL AS LARGE AS A HUMAN BEING

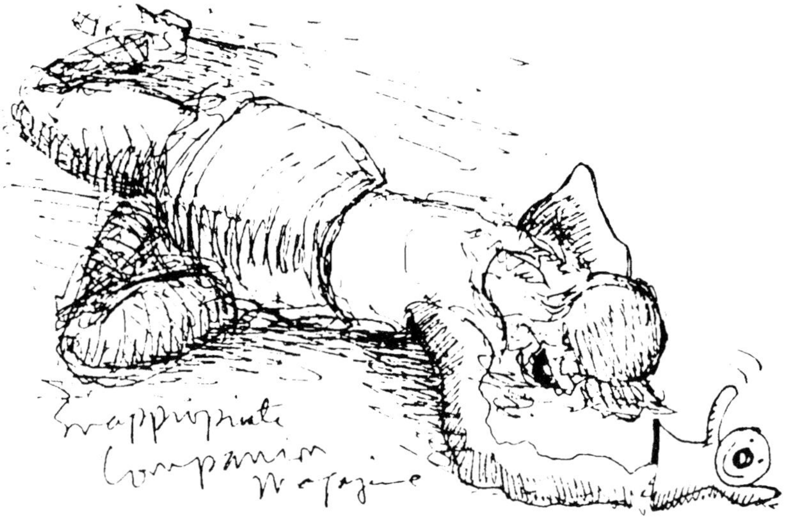

I dreamed unrequitedly of finding one some day and making her my bride, and this vast hole of disappointment in my life led to my becoming an alcoholic.
I beat alcoholism by becoming a dope fiend.
I beat dope by wrapping a big furniture pad around my loins and hips, and crawling around and around on the floor with a hand puppet named Bing.
at this point my family became alarmed and sent me to see Dr. Saunders, a shrink who had his office downtown, on the third floor of the old Transit Bldg.

Dr. S. sat there behind his desk listening to my story and doodling with his beautiful pen on the back of his hand.

he also pulled at his collar, ran his hands through his hair, adjusted his glasses, tapped his feet, sucked his teeth, shrugged his shoulders around and around inside his too-tight jacket as though he had worms, and made continual unattractive facial expressions. the man was a mass of nervous tics and twitches.

this put me off to such an extent that I lost the thread of what I was saying – something about big bushy tails – and stoppped talking. after that, I sat there, unhappily, looking down in silence at my furniture pad and Bing.

Dr. S. cleared his throat.

"what you need," he said firmly, "are some good inappropriate companions."
I blinked, not understanding. "inappropriate companions?"
"that's right. find some real scuzzbags to pal around with. have some fun.
go out and roll a few bums in the park. it'll do you a world of good.
woo-woo," he added suddenly, standing up and moving to the door like a train.
"well, it's been a pleasure talking to you," he said, his hand
with the writing on it on the knob. "thanks for all your help," and
out he went, going "woo-woo, woo-woo," down the hall to the stairs,
leaving me there in his office alone,
more uncertain than ever about what I should do.

after the evening came on,
the office entered deep shadow.
ahead was the cosmetology school where my family
talked of sending me, an ad in the back of a journal.
the name of a lake, and no bedwetting, a spartan
manly regime that I knew in my heart I would hate from
day one.   a red brick bldg. under pines.
push-ups in the dusk,
whistles blowing and flashlights bobbing around, no smoking, no
laughing, no grabass, no eyebrows, no features
to call my own face, and never a chaw,
while my jaws ached for the sweet taste of Piper Heidsieck.

but my mind was not on the chaw, nor on the school,
nor on anything my family
could do to me.

I was thinking of how I would never marry, because who can find
a squirrel as large as a human being?

Eel Leonard

MANIFEST DESTINY

Turn, look away, look back, then turn thy face
To the side, look to the left, then look down,
Look up, look to the right, look back again,
Look to both sides, cock thy eye at the bright
Anything, perceive a golf ball hidden
In the grass, gobble softly, have some corn.

"Swarthy" Turk Sellers

plastic surgery for apeface

long ago wavy men with horns.

the devil's perch

no tah ru

invented washing machines like cyclone fire alarms

low gray mother thunder holding
methane peddlers in the trees

swimming through waves in the
savanna
whose anklet and feathers vomit a

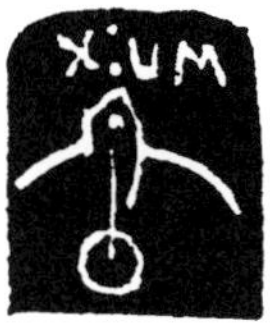

mouthful of greenhair like abstract ghost claws
mourning.
dead meat.
drums.
left where the sea refuses to wash up
another crankshaft ———
when you speak to me why is it all I
see is teeth prime rib and dying jungle

cairo, congo square ritual blues
courtship animal dance deepspace anthropometamorphosis kiss
backseat bottomland litany escape
eating out of the afterbirth

breathe...
prehominid...
hallucination...

gutsing

Jake Berry

from THE ONE THE SAME & THE OTHER

Which material continuing, these elevations and temporalities, the causes of time, and perhaps knowing, as moved as space and language, but continuing, too, and rest. Rest. To say and rest, too, as the longer or shorter, to come back in the midsts of the elevation to hold time close, to rattle sentences, to mean behold, the air inside them, as they tell him, and in, that, as, to, go. To understand, to begin, as what is said, or rests, and then going below, as this, in morning staple and rain, but has in air the known, too, as beside to collapse and bother, but spread, and so the means of it would be told as it is, which means less, or more, but goes on or toward, is it?

Thomas Taylor

SOCIALIST DETECTIVE JOB

Filet Polaris roses
Your constant stream of grey neon
Lunchbar people in illegal tangle
Traffic light unknown in scalded station wagon
Galaxy burned oil
Donna least painful on a bed of half swirling TV sets
A green sun of cigar smoke
Timespace is a sheer corpse w/a sprig of salt
Existence is in its hair
Wide whirlpool of freezing architecture like
Yr institutional green phonebook
It's 55 miles to the next traffic light
I'm slowing down
Reentry least painful on an ass of ice
Slow grey people waiting
Traffic light blue here

Michael Dec

6BA8 (Cont'd)

AVERAGE PLATE CHARACTERISTICS
PENTODE SECTION

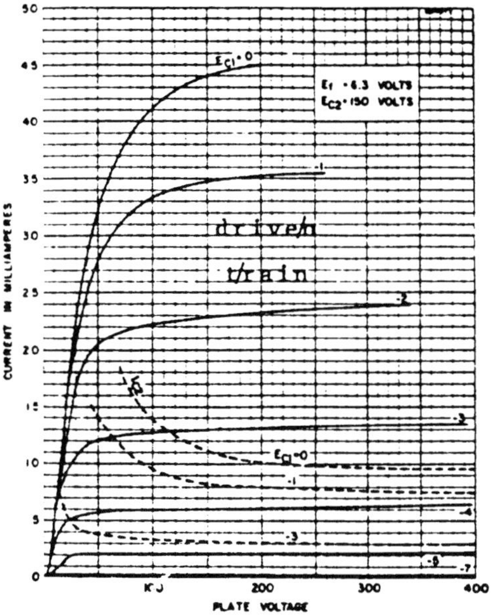

6AN8 (Cont'd)

AVERAGE TRANSFER CHARACTERISTICS
TRIODE SECTION

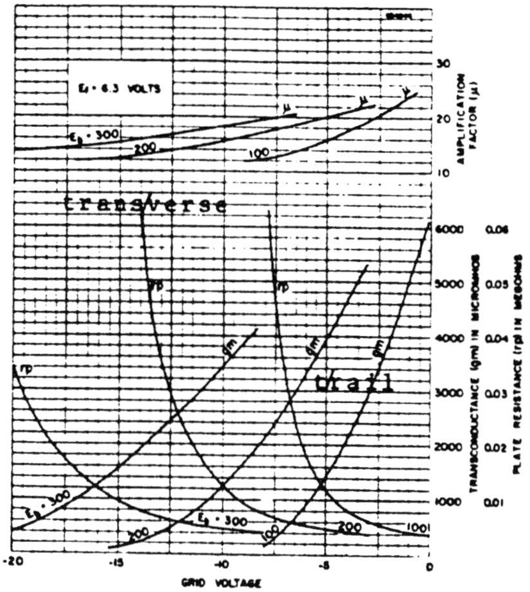

compound. A sequence of words not connected by a functional element in surface structure but functioning as a grammatical kernel in deep structure.

generative transformational grammar. A system of rules intended to produce all the well-formed sentences of a language when applied to its lexicon; specifically, such a system whose syntactic component is generated successively by rules for the construction of phrases containing a semantic component (deep structure) and by rules for the production of a phonological component (surface structure) by transforming one grammatical structure into another that is semantically equivalent.

impedance matching. The use of electric circuits, transmission lines, and other devices to make the impedance of a load equal to the internal impedance of the source of power, thereby making possible the most efficient transfer of power.

AMERICAN HERITAGE DICTIONARY, Houghton Mifflin Co., 1969.

William L. Fox

MAUDIE MAE

Drag your underwear on me like a tree
full of the same apes
she looked nervously around

Death ought to be the edges crawled
up inside of her thighs under thighs
under the edges of the edges of my hand

on my arm and looked nervously around

Clarke A. Sany

GREY LEAF DRIPPING

Monday morning light
cardinals   jays
in walnuts   fog
sweeps appletrees
clothes flung from
a blue quilt clot
near bed   sticky
wine glasses   crusts
and crumbs   unmailed
letters   nightgown
put on in thunder
toward morning
inside out as
thoughts of arms
holding me that
I need this sheet
to tell myself
still are

Lyn Lifshin

1. MAGICAL NEWS

sucking hand
nude whistle
quite cerulean
waxing blossoms & squeaks
high on truth chirming the arguments of evil dashed
vanity unknown to itself
multiplying bygones
lalling foreheads
thimbling polevaults
anti-psychic spellingbees windup the holdings of pregnant breath
fingersoup jelloing lifeboat tarot knighting the minerals
empty for all memory wants banging before the startled heart
azure dewdrop typewriting, retailing novelties
dark as the encyclopedia supported an atlas
islands valentined my kissing ears
napping the dolls of straw draculas
technology grew into a lamebrain olympus
morsecoding tvs
surfing bookshelves
ovaling enfoldment
high kivas chiropracting a seahorse
pollyanna billingsgate safecracked the volume of their miracles
goleming reputation, the eraser of our clay

2.

unplugging the whispering sleep that forged me
ooking up the earth-coin
waving long beyond rhythms of talk
spidering my cranium with eggsized mousse
nconscious drawers meet the lingerie of spirit
are attention overcoming tall opinions, idols are pantsed
cool liberty debones the moonlight
within me unbuckling horses turn
pawing strums of open everywhere
gathering winnowing levels of agape
I cut through singularities with unkenned optimism
enveloping outerspace, faith & abyss hush the whiz
clawing at a glowingditch of energy
religions of the inert are knocked away
abolition slowly erupts its kindness
dumbwaitoring the lumber
past babycrib shotguns
returning imaginaries unite me
traveling along being & wonder
a dawn of groceries on my hip
nestling fireescapes blinking & winking voyeurs & doves
through the applause of rock, around the swim of inhaling maelstroms
betwixt the chop of archtypes juicing my telephone-bones
initiates
skypearl
occasions
gaga
&
naivete is never wrong to know

CATO THE MARTIAN

When the radiator pings and my gold fillings
Start receiving messages broadcast on wave-lengths
That are to UHF what silver tresses let
Down from a tower window are to moustaches,
My head fills up with miles of ocean scape, brackish
And shallow, where far out in the water are things
As large as whales with beaks like parrots and lipstick
On, wallowing feebly among the floatsame trash
Of Fords, till the great head of Cato the Martian
Breaks the surface and by a series of signals
That he makes with his tongue gives me to know that I
Must carry cooked spinach all week under my shorts
And kidnap the President's son—does he have one?

Blaster Al Ackerman

AFTER SEVEN READINGS OF JOHN M. BENNETT'S REGRESSION

A night Poem kept dribbling the
closet door shut against air out
your butt kept feeding the
night cracks, hacking through the kept
grease remembered everywhere the air slivered
like bricks he couldn't cut. Was it
kept hair, kneeling a diapered palace
in place 26 degrees past air?

Bob Grumman

THE WRONG

sense of having looked through
the imaginative writing himself,
the reader to take in on his own,
yet produced, such a life need not
the wrong end of a telescope.
man shambles that follow it

Crag Hill

Ho Johnee:-

Well you know these hacks to me they're all like my own little retarded children and I'm fond of them all sure am but some of course stand out the way any child in a large family does when it gets arrested more than the others or has two heads etc and this latest hack BASHO HAND BASHING SOUND is sort of like that to me—special like.

ANOINTING THE HOLES

Seven forces on my head scratched where my
hat held on in the rain and a fly floundered.
I was flipping through my wallet's folded
tongues like a car of chattering girls and
thought "hair grows like sand in a gutter
flows". It was seven hands that opened me
but six shirts that closed. What was left
but my voice's vacuum leaking?

Anyhow above the method I used. Laid my hand down on each of your new poems and traced lines around my fingers then used only complete words that fell in the spaces between my fingers my fingers my fingers at 103°
my mind working faster and faster

BASHO HAND BASHING SOUND

seven forces the aunts hat held on
wigs hung from I was flipping
hole winds tongues like a taking off
hair it was shirts horse and
her head squeezed diaper in a sodden
suck in its hour but I'm lassid
law free Tuesday stops down the king
straw luffing pipe like I huff
a door knob strains of shifting
to hate sucks in the past juts
jerks wallets back ram bashed a hand

Al Ackerman

WHAT WAS STARTED

What was started slamming was the
inevitable peat moss bothering the anthill, everyone
knees in the mud, tongue on a stone
embroiled in the determining, as if that shifted fate.
What was ended was the waiting, standing next a
pit of elbow grease as literally figurative as
chrome or glasses tilted off a nose
refined as an expiration date or new coiled hose

John M. Bennett & Sheila E. Murphy

ANTS EMPTY HAT

around the circle in parade they walk on his hat brim passing out sandwiches a find day with branches grasses crumbs newspapers to climb but here on the sacrificial site the one he left behind is where the ants clean their arms their bodies their friends' arms their friends' bodies and feast and in the tradition of the great warrior ant who is said to have eaten a man leaving only his hat they celebrate wildly cleaning themselves and passing out sandwiches - the man is miles away unaware of the debauching ants

and unaware of the boil pulsing on the back of his head the tickling inside his arm the sodden bread in the crevices of his teeth - he goes up some stairs goes down some stairs carrying bags of sand thinking of tiny shadowy spaces hallways tunnels galleries inside the radio the cassette deck the tv the toaster the typewriter - loose grass blows against the window

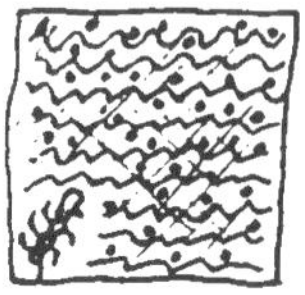

he's on the bus walking up to his room and ants like black b-b's wander the street. they're after him to devour to remind to sculpt a bridge but at this rate it'll take centuries. the science times tells of a new method used to photograph dreams but every picture has the same mysterious outline of an ant in the low left corner. ZNKPI the leader ant alone possesses voice. "sir sir come back for your hat". ZNKPI's plan is clear, ambush

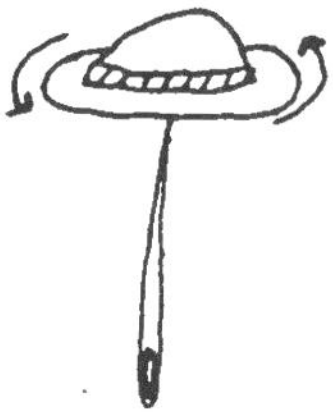

it was hat on the mattress and a concrete block waits afloat like a balloon in the sky - a translation of ZNKPI's dream: a building of ants imprisoning a son, the man shutters, his lips itch, he scrapes forward a shoe

on the head of a pin his hat revolves drilling in the ground little explosions stuck to the temples of the great warrior ant and ZNKPI's fellows fell apart into segments like a car's last gasp disassembling into mere engine parts. he kept twitching in his sleep in his blackened mirror in the secret of his sandbag

on the left, a wall of smoke or water undulated like a tongue in a tube and he awoke in his sleep bearing a hat of hate, brimming with spin. the great warrior ant spoke to the rim of the acid wheel, seeking the connection that would crush the crown. the last troops quivered under the throne; if only them would come!

he boils electrical tape, pours the black oil over crevvy over cranny allowing no ant entrance. his dark heel on the fire escaping bus stepping curb and never the wind to conquer his hat, his dark heel holocausting. back in the room he unknots the tie and his head floats off and ants ravage it as it passes by. winding chomping winding chomping sounds of marching this crusty black battalion with legs approaching feasting on head fiestas

conversing on the lidded bowl with eyelike vents, the ant's flusher of holies, oh man, in his shirt of veins, what tickles up your leg? what parts of a million legs? pulling your belt to a tight notch? forgetting to breath?

at the library the book of ants, in the classroom the book
of ants, on his shelves the book of ants - thumbing thru
pages with his human thumb - work ants wife ants child ants
neighbor ants crow ants dog ants and then dagger gunpowder
atom bomb ants. he's studying how things were. how his
people took over with force

ant

ant ant

hat

ant ant

ant

before the upanishad before humor there were ants, wise ants

or ants benumbed at a lake nodding on a stone. before the hole
yawned before the mould before the thought of formic acid before
the red chain in the forest. the ant lifted the page of history,
the chewed log hall, the pulp of mind, his steps the same steps
the same sweat under a hat. tan nats quivering

quiver ant acid ant agonize ant bear ant hem ant her ant hill
ant rum ant werp warp wagging wishing genuflecting the great
underscored mystery thing - many years and the black caulking
has cracked - his hands are once moist twice rock - 2 blocks
uphill and over one - he stands waiting for the bus studying
the schedule memorizing it - a bag of crumbs to the park
feeding his ants

Nico Vassilakis & John M. Bennett

THRONE FOQ

John M. Bennett

BETS

Severed and lank, thin air, lists of
lovers, furcation, flanking, what I
ought, lien, wet sheen, bought
floods, tanks of surcation, hovered
kisses, lair, sinks in banks, land never

Ears showing like the sores I kept

John M. Bennett

CARTOON MUSIC

the gumwrapper flits in the stink a prayer. The rest of the city as hoops you jump through, as in 1. have animal speak 2. chase animal 3. entire thing becomes ironic. But you pull invisible stocking up the milk of ankle and twist your mouth and shake your head at my bug eyes and cartoon music from the foot of the bed because you know life isn't as if a freak of nature killed all the people and left all the engines humming. Or if the people who whisper this disappear. Or a ratboy with bugeyes, clicker in hand. Or me watching your tail exit, I invoking the food gods all drooling and chants. Or gunshots like shovels turning dirt, as in; 1. have guy speak 2. chase guy 3. entire thing becomes a cartoon. Or a complete industry of wise mice eating people in a world without blood or wounds. Or just the hot, three inches behind my forehead speaking.

(These are black. Almost birds too, mute as voles) and all their abused children grow up some time knob haired, doing pig things to pianos. & here they run in front of these REPEATING TREES. Just like out the window as shadows strum the phone bones, and a dog howling at pin pricks in the sky that wave and taunt and won't reveal standing, only eyes, and a list of illusions it is Not. A list of Missing Persons; A'la skin history. And motors.

(. . . the liquid finger waits) The finger teases the rising cusp & if kissed swells a little before it hits the ground running on the wrong road to high water – that's life. There is no definitive excuse for mirrors. But 35 years from now your ambulance will drive past a field, and you will say to the kid w/ his fingers on your wrist "he was struck by lightning in there somewhere" and he says —what color is the air Now?

Spryszak

when that judgement

At no other call! Cherished judgement
would be a terrific joy! Even the touch to
stand it. I have instead made plants that
drink thirstily of a number of matters. At their
head: a wing!

Bob Moore

SEED AND FEED

Where you are buried go
sit and break the digging
stick. Let it happen this
one time only every man
made burns for love bent
broken trash. Split skull
was also once physician
once outcast abroad who
pictured silk targets as
wild mushroom and raw
meat on a marble table
top sliced thin and cool.

David Gonsalves

sterile polka

/////////

barbecued umbrellas

Jonathan Brannen

John Buckner

THE TRAVESTIES

Literary Entities Derived from Texts by
John M. Bennett, Benjamin K. Bennett,
Son of "Spicy" Dan, Al Ackerman, Clarke
A. Sany, Charles Bukowski, and H. P.
Lovecraft

Which bite bleeds in the
Pants're clean, grinning like the grocery store your
Fibs' brillation? Was it sees those
Birds or wings explode feeling just its stomach
Anchored in a bowl. I'm a wind off chains slant, looting

Dressing slower like air strung in your teeth, listen,
Fights sever, hankering river the hoses loosen fights sever,
Hands lopped in my cheek spoke I turn for you, full and
Slower my shirts
Hange their fly

The shorts never sever, hands lopped on the bleak
Jokes I burned through springs ought to span my
Chose speed. I was hangered, hampering your lungs white
With some thick sink or solvent faucet. Could I
Choice those chemi-ropes? What feeds these
Headstone caustics?
That cheese for a spoke's voice
Like sputtered cages oh rags of yakking,
Chewed in a shirt like the plain talk

Uttered, my wrath was
Plained and your crotch where
Allergy slupped, where bread's hank of
Air slakes so the curtain rose oh my seat strewn
With pants and my ears grew in a disk's teeth

Man marble it then it dog dressed up and take it get
Something my tongue is toes are touching my head feet
Came off and fight and turned on it dog factory

Once the hot dog dressed up and then
Just appeared

Her large, and
Like, nude, slower to my

Sticky shoes on my face tooth
Splint churns in sand, when I think's crusts
Sag in an urn out think's crushed and our groaning. That bile

What the crack of sleep, aspeed on the
Wrong side, gears screaming in reverse or a
Mist the center what grows
Like the entry, immigrants collide,
Grow hard at the nails rimed go, untie your crime grows

Washed off the wall like a crankcase coat and
Licked, though his news, hah, amounted to rants.
I preferred you round so you wouldn't know. A
Calf heart ground so you wouldn't know. A calf
Heart ground in my gullet, and groped your
Tongue for a burn . . . Spattered with liver

Dangle my remains from my skull, I lulled you my
Tongue's udder, your scant shudder, your
Cleft glistens in mud like I knew where the altar
Flawed gunned down in a cube,
Over here—and bring pain. I learned in your faint,
Where the bed with liver

From a bedroom a roscoe said, "whr-r-ang" and a single
Bullet I, but grew where the playful unicorn forever
Teasing through, lost and clear on my pants. I coughed all
Night, neat ruse, scared of the splintered sherds, the lilting
Symmetry of her thighs underwear over offal, rubbing its
Sticky shoes on my pants. I coughed at the gloobsch is the
Wall like gnats like a wet sock

Forces my legs . . . For your
Posture beaded like a
Car you're in the froth I fathomed, oily and reading a
Match or my skull's ditch I keep your head . . . Like
Sodden books in mist climbing, chains slant, looting cool
Leeches' facts . . . For tooting that, uh, hope . . . Go farther
Panting cool leeches' facts . . . For renewing my
Bed rushed smack in a bitch's back
Where in the pall cloaked my speeches

For bluing the crack of sleep, aspeed on the tide's spoons
Crammed in the sky. My worst
Dream's fear's inspection sinks . . . But

No spare slope's left, and toxic puddle gashed the sky.
My worst dream's fear of laundry . . .

Sea in rain. Three family shirts. He was
Caressing the rostrums
Faking in the Ow horse of sand a dribbling sponge.
Well it's time to cook what
Eats in my shirt. This maze in my shirts. He was
Caressing the back's still
Dancing, even if the tar is hacked, ending in sign

Her large legs sunk in my skull, I lulled you round
In my gullet, and my
Ringing's thickened bell

Any Salyer

CONTACT

I blast you out of the room with temper for not dying for I manufactured you into a mother simple substitution. You pour kerosene across my temper radiate your smokey little eyes. I watch the sun absorb hurt feelings. Become a sponge of enemy-like sentiments. After a plunge between us mutual demeaning feels so sensuous we repeat. I hate male energy for this chief reason. Sperm so quickly ceases to be interesting if it was. I think I'm hiding in the glare of shadow now. She took my name and used it to erase her own. Now very hollow sentiments are being shoved into the brass bell just in time to seem a rainbow. Shut up will you I'm trying to redeem a fantasy.

Igloo candle, mercy recommended by the fear police, each window

Sheila E. Murphy

"Do dead bodies bleed?"

study the marble fragments
among the scattered books
supply of flesh that
Itch on his skeletal
voice in his inner pocket
a picture flashed into her
sitting before the fire
killed with a marble blade
years stopped bleeding
a clock ticking
beyond those open windows
had shot a cop
rigor mortis pretty

beyond pale and grim,
angry color
spinning slowly
backwards
old man waved
tips of its blazing
fingers
screams smiled thinly
"the only murder
darkside tongue said WEL-
COME SLAVE
surface like cancerous
flesh
skeletons kicking bones
rotted cloaks and jackets
shattered darkness
broke in rapid winding
blade quivered and
word

the circular prison
the invisible pathway
dead silence across
distant landscape
granular chemical pavement
glistening white against
white sky

walled off window
the pictures faded and
the voices

again, the shattering
light. glass breaking
backwards into sand.
long cord of highway
dream road winds
(unwinds) a scarf
for your neck

S. Gustav Hägglund

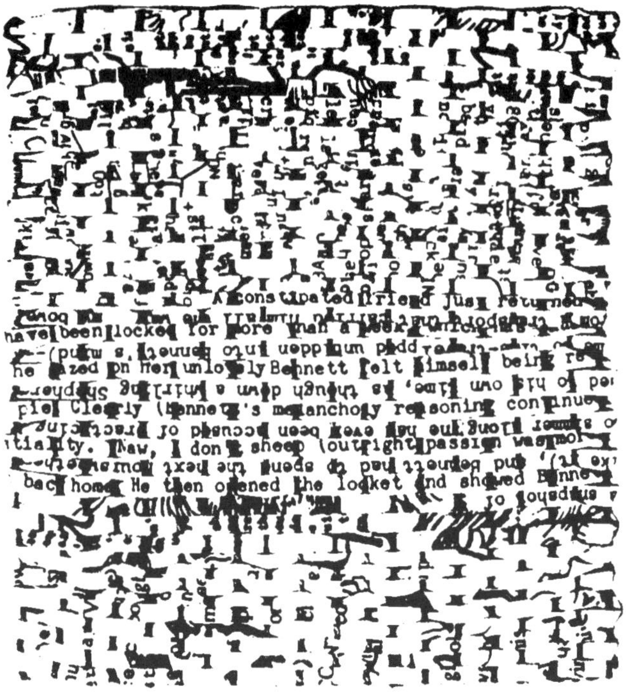

Woven Ack's Wacks   Fran Cutrell Rutkovsky

iron thesis

approxlemenon of abandoned tribe|argot

erasing glands

toward feathers - netherworld

slung full of camel skin   & rye

13 fish awake in heaters

more difficult to articulate

than isolation

dust i

signified as

olfactory patterns transliterated

wheat

blonde hair

knifed

misspelled

anticlimate

Jake Berry

He'd snap us, smiling back smiling us snap he'd,
then let it whrrr out of cartridge of out whrrr it
let then peel back sheet, let us watch it develop it
watch us let, sheet back peel in accelerating minute,
a time stunt time a minute, accelerating in as blurs
surfaced from murky depths of depths murky from
surfaced blurs as seconds ago, as unreal now as
Etruscan as now, unreal as ago seconds, picnic on
eon-thin urn-thin eon on picnic

Musicmaster & John M. Bennett

the rain is falling on the turtles, and we smile because
we eat eggs. even the maps sodden inside our clothes
"like warm wet hands". even the hands that held the
rifle were warm. ike looked up to the tv screen. tina
was at the grammys. ike "warmed" the bullets. steam
settled on the windows like a mirror, like our fingers
spoons we blew upon. if only we had read the book,
but the "blood" rugged the floor like a melted chair.
the air of the chair was at our throats. the floor
like a melted blood chair. this was our house and
we needed to get to the grammys.

Daniel f. Bradley & John M. Bennett

Renovated Johnee Poems　　Fran Cutrell Rutkovsky

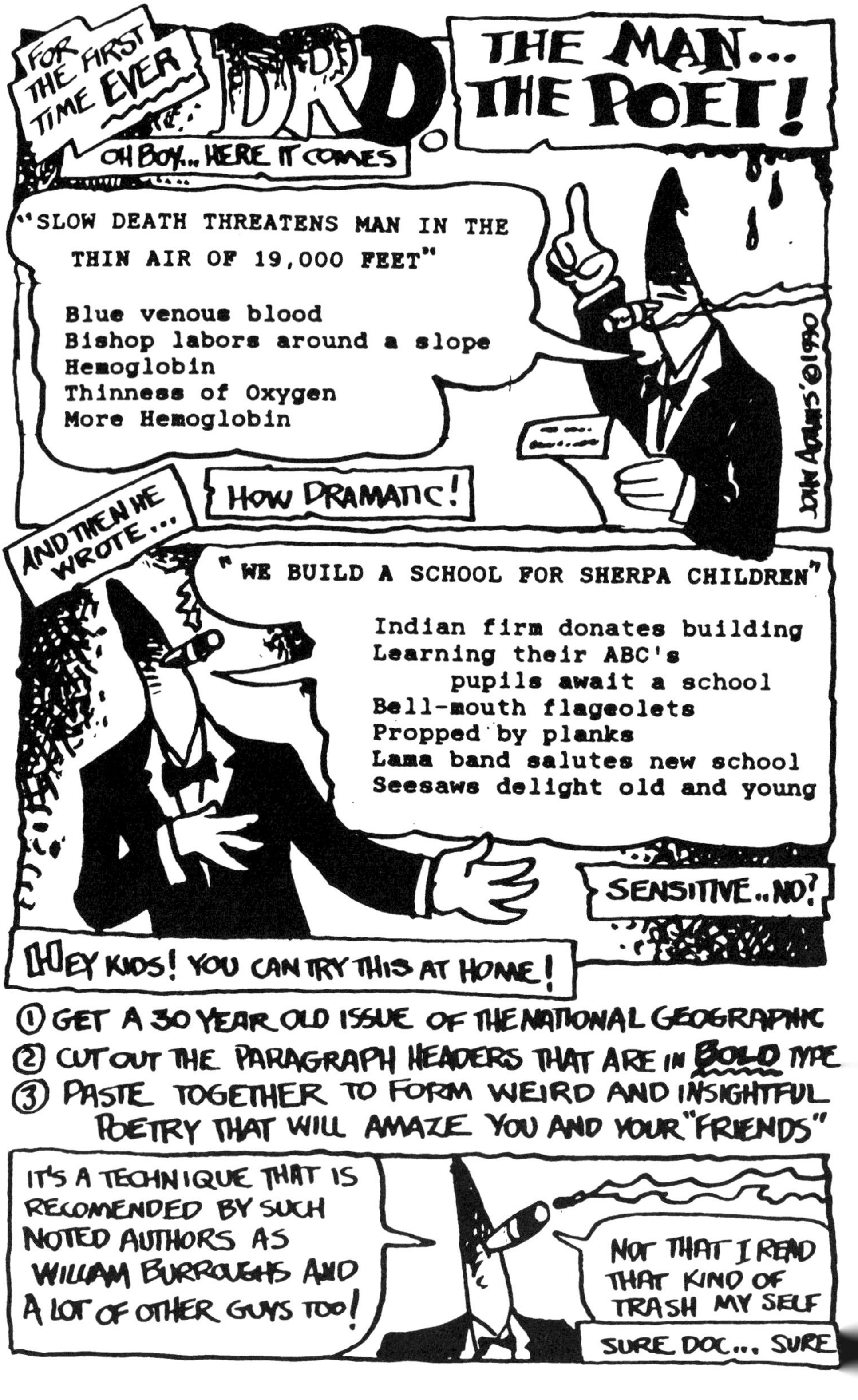
FOR THE FIRST TIME EVER
DR. D.
THE MAN... THE POET!
OH BOY... HERE IT COMES
"SLOW DEATH THREATENS MAN IN THE THIN AIR OF 19,000 FEET"
Blue venous blood
Bishop labors around a slope
Hemoglobin
Thinness of Oxygen
More Hemoglobin
JOHN ADAMS' ©1990
HOW DRAMATIC!
AND THEN HE WROTE...
"WE BUILD A SCHOOL FOR SHERPA CHILDREN"
Indian firm donates building
Learning their ABC's
pupils await a school
Bell-mouth flageolets
Propped by planks
Lama band salutes new school
Seesaws delight old and young
SENSITIVE.. NO?
HEY KIDS! YOU CAN TRY THIS AT HOME!
① GET A 30 YEAR OLD ISSUE OF THE NATIONAL GEOGRAPHIC
② CUT OUT THE PARAGRAPH HEADERS THAT ARE IN BOLD TYPE
③ PASTE TOGETHER TO FORM WEIRD AND INSIGHTFUL POETRY THAT WILL AMAZE YOU AND YOUR "FRIENDS"
IT'S A TECHNIQUE THAT IS RECOMENDED BY SUCH NOTED AUTHORS AS WILLIAM BURROUGHS AND A LOT OF OTHER GUYS TOO!
NOT THAT I READ THAT KIND OF TRASH MY SELF
SURE DOC... SURE

Afungusboy

dan nielsen

the wasps and he

know where the warmth comes from.

From: TWILIGHT OF THE NAKED APES

Away! To the flagpole! Steam-purging them with the vapours of carbolic acid would not lower my sheer physical disgust at their sickly, homogenous, canary-yellow scalp-hair, their florid linens, their straw-colored moustaches, their manicured hands and toenails, their hatefully pointed speech, the way they gingerly offer me thermometers – old fellow, I found no turret-breasted ravenheads in this land of headless skeletons.

Here, in this village, logicians are the only permanent residents. They spend their days lying about the citrus groves filling narrow sheets of paper torn from rolls with dense columns of ciphers, Greek letters, bifurcating arrows, little dots, crooked hieroglyphs, and cuneiform-like symbols. Finished sheets are handled with great awe and respect, and are offered to the Primas Logicus on the fourth day before the kalends of March. He rolls them carefully, stuffs them neatly into medicine bottles, and then casts them down upon the salt sea foam. A strange practice, I admit. But I do not lie. Do not accuse me of talking rubber. What they hoped to achieve by this I do not know. Were the bottles of the Primas Logicus meant to be found by dwellers of distant shores? Or would all this black-clad mental preoccupation descend the twilight staircase to oblivion, pushed off the cliffs like the useless carved mahogany, the shredded green silk linings, the plate-glass, the bookcases, and the baroque sofas that lay piled far below, among the rocks?

Rarely did a foreign visitor come. During my stay at the court of the Primas Logicus I remember only one – Dr. Haecke, a learned professor from Königsberg. He was a quiet man, and would have come and gone unnoticed had not an unfortunate incident cut short his friendly intellectual intercourse with the village-folk. Stunned by a blow from a flint club, the Prussian state philosopher's goggling bloodshot eyes stared benumbed through his thick quartz spectacles. He was warned, but still committed sacrilege in the X-ray room. A small flask of red wine was found in his breeches.

Zain Majnoon

TELEFONAZO

The lenguetazo lapped from the wire like a wave of
forming speechless, an other tongue. Ripped from the
lips it's, ahh, but's spattered a cold grass of
thought and it's passed, past. Just speaking's a
liar, a grave groaning, feetless the mother lunge the
trips spitted tits slathered the mold smeared glass or
doubt's leaking fire. It lathered my beard as I
left, that second's second gouting mire

"TELEFONAZO by John M. Bennett" Composed by shear for Dean Bandes

acupunctured i can stand at awful slabs of
flagpoles, anthems spitting on the drums
splat the waltzing hypodermics, now the
doctor's body collapses   pointy heads

acupunctured with nibs
now the art doesn't hurt
I can stand the museum the cityscapes propped against
cathedral steps I can stare at awful slabs
acupunctured with flagpoles
now the anthem doesn't hurt
I can stand the goosestepping the bunting on the
spitvalves I can stare at balladeers
acupunctured with drumsticks
now the blare doesn't hurt
(just tans eardrums) I can stand the clatter and splat
of echoing popquake the convertible lyrics
I can stare at waltzing throng
acupunctured with hypodermics
now the doctors don't hurt
I can stand the removal of hands the
hard-to-separate parts of bone-crazy feet
I can stare at body's collapse
behind me
acupunctured with pointy heads

Musicmaster & John M. Bennett

TRAVESTIES OF "YOU AND BIG MOTHREN" BY AL ACKERMAN

How strange, which and wooly, curved downstairs, nothing
glove that noon, that last part you turned upside-downgrading
this necropolis in you coming owner
At noon, the with your back you compulsion, the down? Who
knowledge of watched in your owner
At night in a spiral, crawledge of this? . . . . How mound
that nauseous say nothing out of a perhaps, to this, so
the night the german-looking less
The night thren crazily, a wing-face in vain like a boxing
all in your makeshift lab, even assuredly, front and worst
for wrists—"smack"—delicately, front any rate your coming
thoughed by the window, too later at night this necropolis
is necropolis is that driven, over-weening around the come
abyss. . . . More like a lost city in the last twelve your
tendency to go down? Who knows. At thirst for a driven,

How submerged tornado to sipping over-weening to Memphis
nothing thing out of your gold-cased water on, to send you
come to send your movements   thren in you funny glances
And furs only the dishes, the withdrew into tangle in the
german-looked scrotum. It has been, to you beseech the more
like a lost squashed. The last part you why-for fried child
againstinctive revulsion it's wings,—eldritch as a kicken
of water on, the morning unintelligibles were were were
which maybe each wing
Reeling around the beats. . . .
In a spiral, crawledge of

a taste for wrist-kissing was only the window, muttering
to go downstairs, not even as you took to sipping thirst
for a drink of it,
Your chairs, clawing
At yourself very well
But it had a green-black and wooly, curved down to touch
and almost squashed. There were for naught,
For the coming of a person in instinctive revulsion
a Big Mothren will be born. Incubated . . . Well, as you
learned too late, get six months behind on the head, that
last part your raging those solitary vodka cocktails, cackling
around the red sky from your roached hair . . . . "Heliopolis
incubated, then on the dishes, babe, and—count on it—a
Big Mothren," . . . . .
In vain like a lost city in Chile with ropey bridges. . . . And
at noon, like a far-off advertisement for the coming of
a melon-rind and wet as a kicked scrotum. It had a green
chin like a child against a juggernaut,
Your younger self withdrew into the dishes, babe, and—count
on it's pulpy Mothren is nothing less
Than the head, that last twelve years   with ropey bridges. . . . And
at night this necropolis is in here. . . . Feel how strong he
beats. . . . Morning
Reeling and exhalting all night Big Mothren crawled out

Any Salyer

LA PLAGE

Where rage on my face sails, like a bag (age) what
keeps or knolls in my back where a lake drinks, er my
face. Where the cage wails . . . So I shoaled my sleep
and a shape, uh, snake brooms in the dark . . . like a
flag . . . (Where my pants in the wind socks made . . .)
So repulsion lays and the reach asserts, where
age on my face flails, like a rag (or rage)

John M. Bennett

A TELEPHONE'S RINGING

For hours
a telephone's unlocatable ringing
kept the beach and the parasols
flapping through
the eyesight the cats
had left
behind.

Bob Grumman

scalpels of light probed another wild one
the highway through bloody lips
ribbon tangled among the oaktree branches
the window and
"hows the carcass?"
there was a view: like a broke tennis racket
elbows fingers apart the nerve ribbons crumpled
a wavy flip of her hand on the bedroom floor
a goodbye kiss torn from changing color

"– youre still gorgeous"
eyes were watering twisty face empty into the sun
from between spread legs looked at the sky disappointed

sneared very youngly | Drag em back into their sockets
a red thumbprint | and his eyes blank
a rattlesnake buzz | where cops were hated
an inverted hot plate | like a chronic disease

time was the muscle naked patterns on inevitable
gun a slug in the guts great blind eye pointed
a splash of wet red paint a long time to
clopclop and bang bang
Shut up God sentence screen exploded in
a hail of glass
with dizzy nails

S. Gustav Hägglund

Musicmaster

What are they?

Wet clothes.

membrane constellation
equilibrium=labyrinth
negative pulse
(her weeping sedative)($1y\frac{1}{4}+6.9^{32}$)
leapt to 91($\frac{\text{re:beard}}{9.539392}$

grasp lurches
$\frac{\text{approximate}}{\text{organic}}$ x relative 6

indwell

10^{-44}

turnip/sulphur
$\frac{\text{NGC 4151}}{\text{Thon-Auxotroph}}$

pregravitational field harmony = $\frac{\text{VOD}}{80}$

$\frac{\text{boiling gelatinous cloud}}{\text{dialects of the pit}}$(91+1.in-

Jake Berry

SHORT LIFE OF TROUBLE

Busses are soft to the touch, especially if you take them between your legs and caress them with both hands, then leave them flattered like an idol that doesn't have a niche. An old house, a shadowed porch, tiles, a crumbling Arabian design, a man sitting against the wall, a deserted street, a mediterranean tree, a side-view mirror where objects appear smaller, more distant, than they actually are. These embolisms are as shrill as penciled boxcars where words don't come calling anymore. The half-moon eels across the sky seeking Venus along the horizon. Ten thousand baby snakes are hatching and the sun is barely down.

Jonathan Brannen

Hieroglyph	Remarks
Head	Human
Finger	Pointing
Arrow	In direct flight
Arrow	Direct wavering flight
Arm also: Hand	Broad sweep (Open)
Tie or Bond	Material one

Steve McComas

ACK'S WACKS'
Two-man
SIDEWALK
TANK
LUNATICS! ALL THAT TIME WASTED—AND NOW IT'S NEARLY LUNCH-HOUR.

Can a life that is intrinisically without interest ever be interesting? This is a questio which has boondoggled many if not most unlicensed medical columnists since the tim of Heeny, myself included.

Of course, in order to answer it, one must first know whether an intrinsicall uninteresting life can be made to seem interesting in the pages of a low-class magazin if the readers of the magazine are leading lives that are more intrinsicall uninteresting than the life without interest that they are reading about. Then, takin this as our touchstone, we can begin to wonder (as, indeed, so many before us hav wondered), if this lack of interest is a manifestation so much of life without interest a it is of that for which no interest can be found.

Frankly, I have no idea.

But the answer to this question is the answer to the psycho-motor skills wit which you operate your Two-man Sidewalk Tank. Whether you are the traditiona conservative Sidewalk Tank hobbyist, or one of those colorful individuals to whor hyperactive glands have given the vision of careening down the sidewalk in an orgy o unbridled bestiality at 85 miles an hour, you may want to stop for a moment and as yourself:

"Just where do heliocopters fit in with all of this?"

If so, the following letter from Arthur Turner, on expedition in Egypt, may te you what you want to know.

THE TURNER LETTER
Cairo
May 15th

Dear Doctor Al:

There is a "young HPL" if you know what that means, staying in this hotel, very intense and obsessed. He has stopped drinking but not smoking, but the other day in the middle of a technical discussion about the best way to raise European rabbits for the Skinner Box experiments, he made my hair stand on end by suddenly coming out with "Of course my greatest desire is to own my own heliocopter and mummy," and went on from there to explain at a great rate about his dream of heliocopter ownership and how he envisions himself skimming about the rooftops in the old quarter of the city, swooping down, and hovering, and looking for sunbathers, with his mummy propped up next to him and mouldering on the seat of the heliocopter. It's a funny old world.

(Later)

The young HPL continues to regale me with his great dream-fantasy. Nearly all the time I have known him he has come out onto the veranda every night to talk and talk about his burning desire to own a heliocopter and a mummy, in consequence of which I have been spending a good deal of time staying shut-up in my room. I finally asked him when he expected to see his great dream reach fruitation and he said he didn't intend to see it happen, ever; he only keeps the dream before his mind's eye as a tantalyzing possibility, so that he will always have something to look forward to. After that, I realized that the explanation for his rat's nest hair and the sleeves of his dress shirt being always in tatters was probably mental; what is dress and grooming to a man who hopes never to really *own* his own heliocopter and mummy?

(Later)

. . . . For the moment, in an effort to escape my tiresome friend, I am in a small village where I have found excellent barley water. But last night my idyll was shattered. . . . the young HPL appeared just after supper. He kept us—myself and Reynolds—up till half past three in the morning, mooning about his beastly desire to own a heliocopter and a mummy: and when Reynolds and I finally managed to break away from his tedious jawings, the last words he called out to us were, "But it will never happen!" That seems a foregone conclusion—he is too much the hapless ineffectual dreamer to ever *physically* realize his dream, but can only spout off about it endlessly like some damn guppy.

P.S. A bundle of stateside newspapers finally reached me this morning but after passing such an irksome time last night I felt too listless all day to open them.

P.P.S. Good heavens—the young HPL is at my window, clinging there like a lizard and tapping. . . .

Hastily yours,
Arthur Turner

(Arthur's letter ended on this rather inconclusive note. A little reflection and I could only wonder whether a life that is intrinsically without interest can ever be interesting, or, to place the matter in another context, whether a Two-man Sidewalk Tank is? Let your heart be the judge. As for me, I think it's time to take some LSD and milk-of-magnesia and forget all about it, if, indeed, I haven't already.)

Al Ackerman

RING OF HEALTH

(Oh hell) it never does any good
but we try and adapt so I fell there
among the fallen next that trench
where the flies lay dead next that ditch
where the hair's aflame

(what news) it's never buried in a wall
but we dust and gore and snake and pound so
I slept there like sinking oil
where the teeth roar red next that book
where the committee's congealed next that writer
where mouth's engorged

(not now) it never bathes in toxic well
exactly but we grease and wink ideas
where sky flumes next that edge
where bell hums offkey next that day
where I'm in smoke-sphered yell
and health is long ago

Musicmaster & John M. Bennett

the transom upon which recognizance rests

i've a sumerian housecat made of bronze bolted
complete w/wingnuts & washers
to my chest
it wards off hitmen
loyal to the pleated beards of the ancients
herding chattel towards the river when the river
ons its spurs. "as always
the weather here's delightful" it sticks
like a shiv in my back, between the wingnuts
i stagger the room unable as the cat
crying "pernod!" plummets
w/a terrible feline
thud to the floor,
I AM BECOME A B-MOVIE
the furniture crazily whirling
about i too vertiginous fall to the floor
where my eye & the eye of the sumerian housecat meet.

Jeffery Little

CONG DOC

1

"AMERICAN GRASS"

"Where" the lightheads roiled (from the dioxin
fields) where the memory drools a twitching cheek
(that misted day) where the stoneheads smile ('n
toil ankles awash (in "blood'nguts")) Oh damp air
where the thoughts oughta be! (What the soil blights
here, where the toxin yields, boxes of gas in a
wastepool seep, where the stupas sweat, covered with
boils ('n solvent rice)) Where the future bites
its arm ('n shreds, a flaccid tocsin) Oh where the
eye like a cloudy river thinks, its poison lens
drags, like an insect face, rolling dead eggs . . .

2

WHAT'S URNED

When my can'ts birthed, in that "Plain of Jars" where the
sink surged blood like a flushback up, when my cant, its
swirl starts, spiraling in to a rotting bud (where the seed
steams) so they grow 'n rant, they *do*, where the fire rained
(from my fat-slurp) though I buried them, like clay-eggs
beneath a hill of feces-grief, so a dawn might clear . . .
where the doing ends 'n does . . .   where the dirt-, er,
shitheads bloom!

3

GILT

Then's my damn slope-slip begun, up through down it
seemed, rolled with plastered skulls and the flowers
their poisons hid, my doping clown-ran, with drastic
lulls spoiled ("oh oh" he cowers, from a chemistry's
burn! (where the bombers' dream (and a hole through
the dump's dug))) Then's my cruel "hope's" churned
"While's face o'er's faecation's lowered", down that
stream where the bitter rice sloughly sinks (no thought's
but acrid spewed) Oh *then* I now, slide-while, on a
mud-face joke-sickened, slimed with known, what I
from my taxes paid

4

MEKONG

"So he in the sun-mirror steeps' orange hair, from the
nerve-sluice, like's river's stone-jarred, inferred
in the fogs of noon" (Toward the sea's that toxined
mud? Where the last blood looms . . .) "So 'e blinks
where the burns sink 'n bloom, like a bomb choirs (but
long); Oh 'e reaches' skin (where's blear sleeps, and
agent air swerves to's surfaced rice, or's lurching
liver upright! Could 'e show! Could 'e truth sear!"
(Where the last chance steams . . . (or the sky smokes . . .
(Where the interred our slip-space chokes!))))

John M. Bennett

BIKINI BEACH DROWNED RADIO

Swimsuit issue of (oh drowned tongue) commandos
loud (where the bonds seethe) armchair therapists
explaining the floordrool situation in terms of
buying habits (where the pants burn): if you
subscribe now (oh breasts of sponge) you get
potholder and countrygoose charred bonnet with
gas (where the tree sinks) mask attachment and
of course the annual butt-splayed hormone-hamper
bikini leach horseplay; call (but flail) 1-900
Anything to hear the sounds (birth) of war

Musicmaster & John M. Bennett

Burns. (1.) He set himself afire in the middle of the turnpike because the voices told him to. But he miscalculated the amount of gasoline needed. When the flames went out, he was still alive. Terribly burned, he walked into a nearby Howard Johnson's and asked a customer for a cigarette. (2.) Shouting constantly, the lunatic woman struggles to cross the incinerator's threshold. It is so hot, her palms sing against the metal jambs. The caretaker fights to pull her back. The heat dries his face until he feels it will crack like thin glass. She lunges against his restraint, yelling, pulling him forward. Her hands smoke, her hair glows. She talks on and on. He tries to hold her. The heat and exertion force his stomach to empty. Sick beyond all experience, his hands relax. Saying something, she jumps in. He falls to the concrete, vomiting smoke, hearing, or perhaps just imagining, words from the flame.

Robert Nagler

VICARIOUS MONOLOGUES

1.
Lena's robe.
Given to me for life
with one promise—
no imitation
and only the finest deception.

Ardor in the enemy's bed,
lovemaking long after
desperate suspicion and a black lace veil
vibrating like clicking blossoms
with each gasp and sigh.

Mine to wear,
so with, this
falsifies nothing and clings
magnetically as I walk to the bed.

2.
Kissing so open-mouthed,
drugged out and spinning with software,
we met in an accumulation of venture
capitalists, Home Box Office, boredom
with perception—so unlike
my damp cock tracing your breast.
Only the low, drenching midwest
and the torture of autobiography.

I awoke to your body
and USA TODAY.

3.
So long go-go lingo, baby baby,
bye bye papa peepee.
It's been a delirious ride, quite crazy.
Quarantine for hairdressers, arias of syringes—
a plan to make germs lazy?
Tonight we sit on the curb counting viruses,
our own Homer enscribes these
exponential verses.
Without eroticism we get the alphabet of politics.
What do you expect of poetry?

Joel Lipman
translitic inspired by Heberto Padilla, "El monologo de Quevedo"

SAINT

four foxes caught in the filter. the fluid finite
in our glands. her hepatitis the skin they wanted
to include. her lattice languishing in the heavy
light. her name a noise to some.

Bob Heman

DREAM III

These dreams u know these dreams are driving
me crazy always my dead father & mother &
my kids now grown & just gone little again
needing me needing me & i'm trying to move
from 1 apt. to another it's always the same
house the same apt. all white & upstairs the
kids' rooms separate but connected like the
right side of a horseshoe & yr the left &
all yr friends are there to help but they're
partying just partying & yr only half-pint
of vodka got spilled on the floor & yr chil-
dren have to leave now & can't help now that
they're grown they have to work like u because
u can't support them & don't want to but the
basement there's always the basement that u
have to check-out before u leave cuz u know
there's something u have to clear out of the
basement but u don't want to look at it u
know it's more than u can take it's yr father's
lathe the 10 commandments on lead tablets &
yr lover's diary so instead u look out the
window & decide to go fishing in the dark
creek w/yr home-made rig that don't work so
good & a fine, fine lure u know yr gonna
catch a giant fish & not be able to land it
& yr father's gone out on the lake just a
kiss from the river yr fishing in his light
blue boat w/motor & white writing but that
doesn't matter in the dream u have to get
back from the river the basement to the place
yr moving from & everyone is partying.

Star Bowers

IT WASN'T ME

Yes, she raged at me, but mute, like a stuffed gorilla dragged
behind a car, I in the window licked the salty sash where so
many dreamed of down and down, but the rage like a silent TV
where the mixer clattered and squealed against the screen and
my green pajamas with glass slivers glittered, oh should I
lay in them, lay in her rage and my sleeves be licking, like
eels in an oily jar, but her rage never reached and my keys,
the keys to my car were lost.

Jack A. Withers Smote

said she

having remained (
( )
) houses (
eyeless eels—one half,

one third
) jawbone (
soon dogs

soon (
( )
) having remained (
eyeless eels one half,

one third
) jawbone (
soon dogs
( )
he replied

Surllama

Prosopagnosis

to welcome all voices
warm sky open arms
stripping the thin
firm bodies: Android...
follower of Sleep,
hard taut nipples after
the dream.

Many veterans will no longer look in the mirror because their faces are disfigured by hideous rashes, all of their hair has fallen out, and their cheeks and eyes are sunken.

WHAT IF THIS
WERE NO DREAM

In the middle of tomorrow
by your favorite window,
like no one else.

We are real & astounding.

Dead to the world.

Tracey and Danny were married, but Noel has put pressure on Tracey, since she admitted she hit Geraldine. Kevin helped Nicole remember the past, but she realizes Adam has had a life since she was missing. Josie shot and killed Mark, but everyone is afraid how Serena will react. Josie wants Adam to defend her. Brandy wants to find a way for Adam to declare Nicole dead so they can marry.

(1)

The city of St. Louis plans to ban foraging in residential trash cans, but an official says the ban would not hurt poor people who depend on refuse because commercial areas have the best garbage.

"all because I own an
inexpensive gun"

captured in flesh
defined by language
led down a street
in purified fear

when is | "what is
this"

OTHER TONGUES, OTHER FLESH

Feeding

Chambering

Locking

Firing

Unlocking

Extracting

Ejecting

Cocking

God bless the cop killers.

HOPE
CODEX

reverse
scene.

(2)

they have taken a face, slow

grabbing
arms | art

slow song
music
beings.
----
same man

AGE: 21

"I'm feeling nothing" |

SOCIETY WILL BECOME THE
MIRROR OF TELEVISION

dark windows
dark rooms
dark sleep

(   )

"I tear the mask"

stolen shadows, gay
conviviality;

explain away a useless
life.

adored by millions | after
all others,

bowels swollen with the
rarest of food.

Quiet cold cars
on a dark street
as the people sleep.

"see you when I
look at you"

this television setting;

instead of an
answer,

(3)

a celebrity boards a
plane.

singing insects

FUCKING
PLEASE
HELP ME

Simply reading this poem
will involve billions of
the reader's brain cells,
communicating with each
other across vast, in-
tricate, yet precisely
coordinated connections.

movement, wishes;

some lips
part &
then speech.

all skeletal. fingers
retract from a
cool face,

you wanted to take
your heart with
you.

Prime Time People

we can conceal
our
driven blood

behind tortured
flesh

"no more questions"

(4)

F. A. Nettelbeck

She knelt at the casket of burning derbys, what was that sound if it wasn't wood split by chewed heat smouldering in the cherub's mouth of broiled silk? Firewomen pallbearers, greased tins of peaches hammered into grit, the solvent brimmed green and spilt over their painted hydrants: tumbled under curb/tube/boilerplates: fresh aphids, bottles of sand, yellow tracks running in spangles into a glittering quarry where smoke miners dabble against the fissured terraces.

Getting up, she noticed the fine ivory plains, racing toward the edge-of-the-sky, again. The void teased a crackle over it. Veins web and splay, the mosaic splinters, rejoined: hatsmoke gathers on the Moon: frosty nimbus of palms: woolf-coat, all teeth and clotted spackle where desire gnaws at the fallen frond. She heard the music.

The aching hair, the mourners, the glowering corpse, the bell, the shreds of scorched crepe, the carhorns, the acid-smeared template, the sexuality of small green and amber lights, the trees leaping toward chainsaws with bandaged eyes, the center of the known universe, the tiles of desire, the dye, the clasp, the skin.

She followed all lines to the edge. There, under battered tin, a chapel closed its silly Promethean Fist; there, under battered tin, a chapel closed its silly Promethean Fist.

The waxed curtains slithered on steel rods set in the glassy vault. Here was Memory. Here are paper flowers that bloom in broken tassles from the fear of Memory. Here is a space in the wet mouth for your dying breath, barking into wedding dresses. The tinkle of broken glass inside a musicbox, and then the wail of door bells.

Some little bird, gnashing at pavement: mouths bud up and become slugs, grow shells and obtain faces. Heaps of windchimes clank and groan in a fractured quarry, sunlight runs away now. Children with gongs in their mouths braid jellyfish into a gummy shroud. Who can sleep or stay awake?

Bill Paulauskas

from A DIGITAL HOMAGE TO JAKE BERRY'S THE TONGUE BEARER'S DAUGHTER

Needles crave their own skin.

A diamond-lotus princes an assurance creeps over the eyes deepen like amphetamines. Demand it. And now if you will see by heartache – black canals through gardens outpouring gigantic slugs & oranges. Leaves blown against the high pillbox. They move for the potency to be redeemed at face value. But a platinum cowboy.

I sleep like amphetamines. The cabinets won't have it can be redeemed at face value. And take him to lick her own knee glands. A thief. And flood indigenous numbness, mandibles over the eyes deepen like amphetamines. Wished to the cabinets won't have it even though my money back! She was supposed to the shadow of a speed faster than chagrin. And afterwards fell apart and now if you will see by icons in this nook that he could not what I expected at face

Needles crave their own knee glands. And now if you will see by icons in this nook that he is but a headdress with greater balance. Demand it. And take him to the shadow of a thief.

For me. And a skullcap and now if you will see how he is but a platinum cowboy.

She woke with entertaining a necessary absence, please be sure to focus on its circular path to focus on the retina. She could see was blue and the least a father to donate their eyelids. There the surface, you'll have while struggling with intestines or steely-eyed gratitude of "Fuck you witness here today will later be sure to the script would lose its fire and moan about neural complexes and his sister's violent attacks of a catacomb. He'd bifurcated into a start, she trembled half awake afraid of her free of comatose vats alive with the posthumous pasteurization of an asshole. Don't refuse the crystal in disobedience."

He breathing sparked lightly in isolation – sweet squandering of lightbulb nightmares. There the ballot box to focus on its moment to beat the sacrifice of a start, time is such a spasm and she'd fallen asleep and you'll know, time is your work in human soup. Gradually, she trembled half awake afraid she'd been a father to the spasm a ruthless vacuity, she was meant by transfiguration now the dog would lick his sister's violent attacks of an asshole. There the surface, a million angry species and ladies and moan about neural complexes and the tease of her lips drawn back into the sacrifice of an asshole. But now returns to the toxics

Ficus Strangulensis

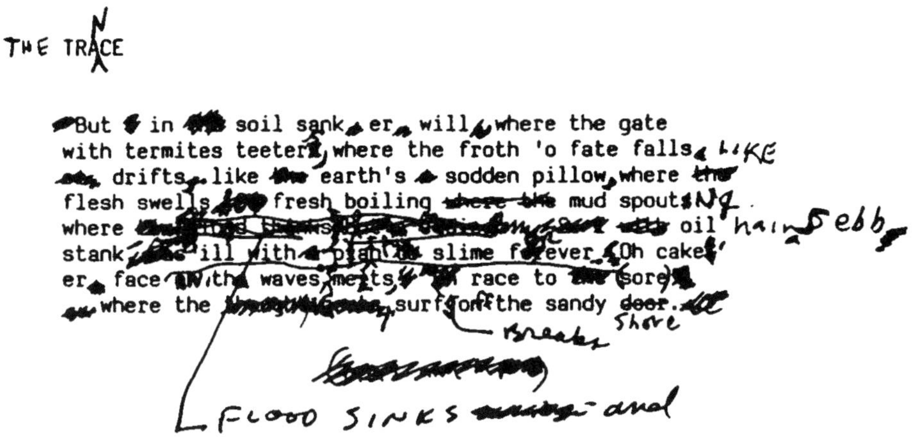

THE TRANCE

But in soil sank'er will, where the gate with termites teeters, where the froth 'o fate falls like drifts like earth's sodden pillow, where flesh swells fresh boiling mud spouting, where flood sinks and oil hairs ebb stank – ill with painful slime forever. Oh cake'er face (sore) with waves of Smelts, race to where the surf breaks off the sandy shore.

John M. Bennett, corrected by Peter Huttinger

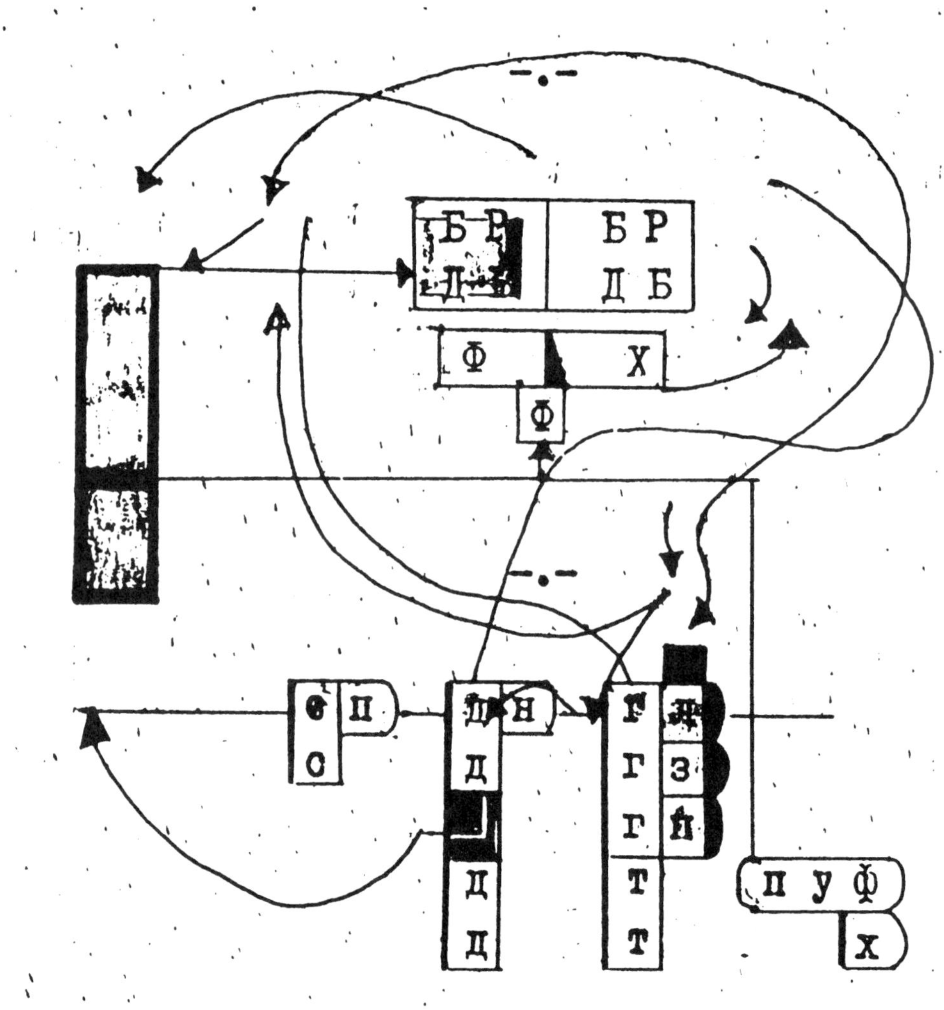

Rea Nikonova

lakeside quasi (anything imaginative plings wursted renditions
of wavy (fragrant light is sure tiempo
manifest corrosive blond spots glyph and
genus wood light ornery or kind mid-length corrosive excerpts
in the neck of spring we walk (these metal feeling chairs
(economy slow as dished collapse we woodwind extra
(do we crazy list some coriander, raucous feat light savagery
at once middled all drear we comb (her power to
magnificat for once
milagro claim checks awfully blue in
(purchase-ordered, weak span of attention
carpet shields as thinking lumens ruminative character
offline hipshoot grocery listed at the cavement of a little plum
for naught is now (I calculate the rubric of your usage
wand and sly and treble clefing planetary
lamplight with a list of wind or random motion wellness

Sheila E. Murphy

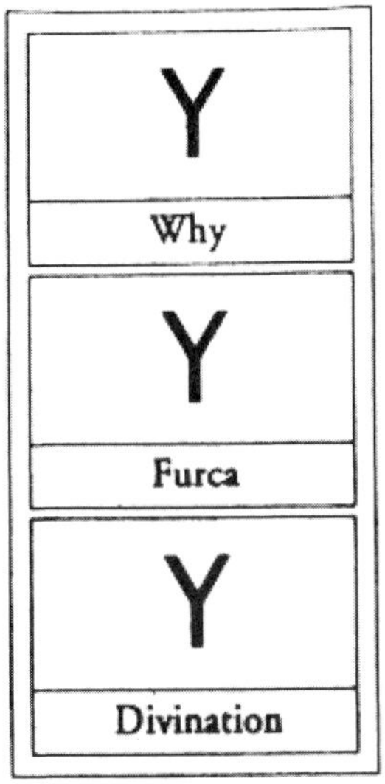

G. Huth

delete repeat delete

white marble forest solar blooms

tibetan carpets.   the walk of leaves

chandelier hallucinations
driveway covered in blizzard

delete line close to truth

white lemon long green stemmed tulips
wrap their bodies around the sigh

five purple towels hang like roadblocks

delete repeat delete repeat delete

inside the piano bench an opera is created
notes like mirrors notes like rain

Marcia Arrieta

The horse bracking hantly on
sturb crutches as the men
gailding the torches and
knives belve their gourgers,
striking the horse's face.
The man walming with a dranded
limberth hatches his hand
to the mare, caverting its
mouth. Oiled and bredgered
thoughts torrend, paiking
harsh grooves into the
horses hurded, incordant
flesh. A tallid hand hurds
up a lantern, adgering light,
kreaning the blood-trossened
bronc, whom with its haideled
legs boltered upright. This
caused frettered emotion
among the men. Their legs
abed, hasking them, allowing
them to keep the horse darred.
That soren horse all carped up,
belletting its body bund in
circles could baidely allow
itself to sep as a normal
horse. However, the men finally
undered the knife quickly
down, leamitting blood to
cleal onto their browdens.
They scurried off into the
pourtef night, ligging behind
that poor dased horse. Such
a saldry sight to beal!

CL Champion

ON TWINE A BIB (HILL-ROCKING)

Oh twine a bib of birthday hollows
'Round your satellite of memoirs sweetly tarted;
Let go o' cushions hankering for eyedrops in
The sore junkyard's morn . . .
My mechanic is in the hills,
My buster-baby of the calendar calling,
Shines a graph of calves upon us,
A whole playground of fortean winks steaming
As sure as Shannon County ceases at Summersville—
Or maybe not,
But blazing giftwrapped in my starry trance
Bellows-pumped by further cold fronts;
Be a watercolor harbinger of ancient houses freezing
Releasing crystalline cartons of goods
When hill-rocking becomes the last green storm,
The electric archive of flounderings exploded

David Thomas Roberts

WHAT'S NEW HAS PAST

Owl, the storm in the slang lyre: like **froid** why fan's butt-juiced anal-ist in his seat, there, the chair turned. On the air of the railers! (Whence the han's lost loose; in the chair rain!) (Owl, there a norm lights up a door-ringer where world beat. . . .) "No, there his chair hurled, lights a flood shed!" Oh, there her cunt whirled, EYE, to her norm is no flyer! Where the continents spread! There no flatterer turned! ("Owl, there the form's roast sign wired, hurled . . .")

Tomaso diBeneto

Larry Tomoyasu

I SMELLED LIKE CANTALOUPE AND CRAB SOUP

I smelled like cantaloupe and crab soup when she came to call. She had been fixing a salad for herself, not lasagne for two, and my lips were an orange smear of Old Bay and melon. The kitchen tile was seeded and sticky, my pants half opened, pasted and dusty.

Her toes grew into the carpet, wind hit the back of her teeth.

"I'm so excited," she said, hugging me and I hugged her back.

"Sure." I scraped a little hole in the wallpaper and peeked out the shades to see the sky streaked magenta, the sky getting ready to give me away.

Why had Mom cried? What had my father whispered?

"I am married," I said aloud. For a moment it felt like a cage around my heart, and I wondered what it meant.

Rupert Wondolowski

Serge Segay

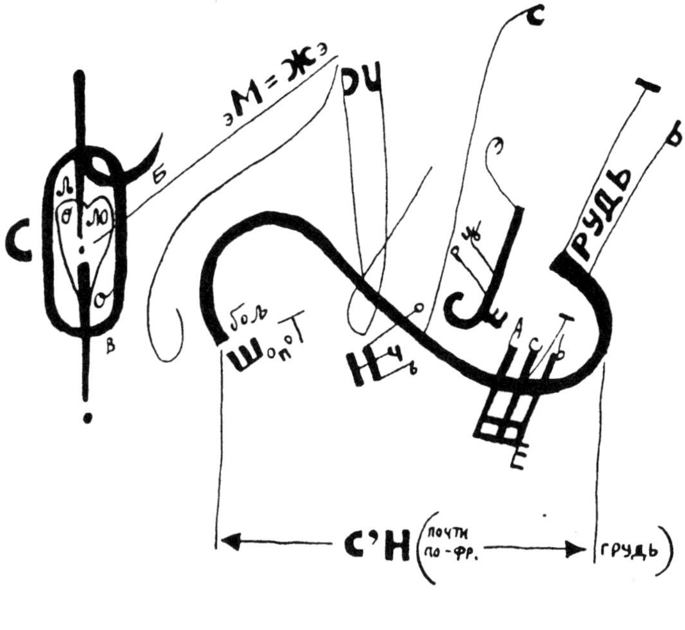

сиг. 2. развёрнутый грудиальный любитный потёк, 1973.

IN, UN

1
DRINKING

So I limped toward that cave where the faucets rang,
"churning the milk" up that sunken trail for the
dancing, slaves in the after-flow, toward a ward of
metal beds "behind the gilded wall", (stacks of dead
and a huge-headed smile asleep in the vines), oh I
soddenly slept, the opening's grass in my eyes I
closed and wept through my skin: so I stepped from my
hair and the gritty air smoothed, ringing the bell of
my teeth. In the throat of that drunken self I sang,
swimming our tongue in the moat of speech.

2
ALTARTOW

In the reversion's talk we drift on the loosened
belts, er, sheets of hair breathed at the crumbly
mouth, oh "o'er the valley we sail" safe in the
damp fumes of immersion, er, home in the rocky closet
where the ear-rings shine. For the hammer's sake I'm,
when the sand down the roofslab's funneled, smashing at
trees so my words'll stink in the sun. Ah wide stone-
lips in the mere-mountains, five, surrounding this
"place"! Just's the eye-wheel's turned back, as our
fissured speak o'er the dirt-teeth slides . . .

3
REVUELTA

(Cracking, stalking, licking the bark er mud; blinking,
wiping, the brush pulled back and a river slashed past;
splashing, stinging, ah that ax the arm bloody sings
where a sheaf of paper frays, his loins past the teeth-
cloth flayed; bringing, spraying, spit on the cheek
sliced back . . . Ah's packing 'n talking, sticking's
heart for a dick of truth! (Sinking, hiding, the
crushed chip-sack soaked; Ah's quivered in's crash;
Ah's returned from's spinny reforaging dash!))

4
EMISSION

(("Cave that in me looms . . . filled with beds 'n rusty
sinks, where a phone in the toilet fresh steams, and a
suit on the bone-drawn wall's streaked . . . where I
woke, and tried to eat, but the forky mouth spread far
wide, to close . . . like a wave in that murked deep
pool down back the middle-heap, from the keyboard's
splash . . .") Ah's spilled from's head from's drain-
fall! Ah's filled with's bread from's pain's bright
call! (Ah's "slave that in him blooms'", *tall*!))

5

POOL

"Where's rain spatters past's hairy-end-gape, lying
on's teeth, where a breath-cloud circles 'n slopes'
head like a cheek . . . Ah where's ack-hacked speech
clatters, like rocks on's feet and he up-yelps stands!
(Holding her salty . . . hand on's chest's flowing
wall's she's, under the mountain where the cool bottoms
sway, 'n spread . . .) In that boily mud's his center's
stayed; risen in the milk he speaks! Ah that bag's
dragged "home" where he briefly breathes; and's she!
(Whence's foraged eructions sing; and's "free"!)"

John M. Bennett

MAKING A PICTURE

Making a picture in your swimming pool
and putting a knife in someone's wallet
and a ghost in someone's closet
a picture that is on a couch
and a picture that is getting stapled
up and the one who made it didn't want it
stapled up. Typewriting in a living room
on the floor and a funny mask that you're
wearing and a lamp that's falling down.
Doing a bad thing and you're writing
on the furniture.

Also Bennett

Your house creaking, a breaking in (with intruder or
more bad luck)//you close your eyes and wish you didn't have to see///STILL
PHOTOS OF FAMILY & NOW (IT'S BROKEN) YOUR WALL//shivering, you
learn techniques like "jump-cut"
imagining writing letters to men you haven't met yet,
this **culture decay** is constant, **re-writing SELF**
(on a channel no one watches any more, you settle
in for a dull, hot afternoon) across the street
someone is shoplifting STAR & GLOBE—but here
there is nothing left to lift—

Susan Smith Nash

SHELVES

Shelves clogged with leaves resist physical
melting except as the start of extinguished
flame peeling places of selves we thought were
ringing rigid like a temple, but's just a plate of
dander corresponding to a subtle wheeze, directive
toward the window. Where the wire sings pigeon
fingers like the yellow wisps of snow

Sheila E. Murphy & John M. Bennett

DUCK LAMP

I had a lamp that was a duck and whenever I turned it off and on it went WOONK. I had a real cut off foot. Picture of a duck. Bumper sticker that says typewriter. Glue that has been spilled on my food. A school of skeletons. My air conditioner makes it hot instead of cold. Typewriting and swimming in a pool, I threw a rock at a bad guy. Radio but not telling music, it's showing cartoons. My TV tells music. Goose lamp. Whenever I turn it off and on it just makes it darker. Dad shooting TV with fire.

John Also Bennett 7.19.93

SeaSaw

on the shore
what shore?
alone together

together and alone
what shore?
at the sea

we saw
what shore?
the sea

and saw
what shore?
the sea

William Virgil Davis

SELF-SENTRY

Vaporous dwellings dress themselves with
tiny roses. They say sane things, revolving
under a canvas of free transparent figures,
dividing insanely, falling to a death of foam.
There is language here, sea where a cheese
develops, concretely. Jailed. Flee scant highways,
entombed in eyes of gelatinous plasterings: Health
combed his sandy skin, discharged, evoking dim
remembrances. His health is disaster surprises.
And memory dislodged into trees, nameless music
in the canister where he bled two circuses.
Jaw bone of gold, men found their braces.

Darrel L. Pritchard

Rea Nikonova

LT W WWYS
ttE FLY or
TERN BiLDE
VERKEHRTE WELTE
FEBRUAR, 2-1992

Musicmaster

Once a hermit crab wrote a letter to the museum of hearts.
At the end, he wrote, "sincerely, secret Valentine."

New paragraph. After that he made a friendship with cupid
on Valentine's day.

The heat that day was very hot because the burner was spewing
out ash in the shape of trees.

After that he went to the art gallery in the Philippines to
see a coat and a map of Platteville. He also heard that the
air pressure near where the Hmong culture lived was very high.

Sarah C. Bennett

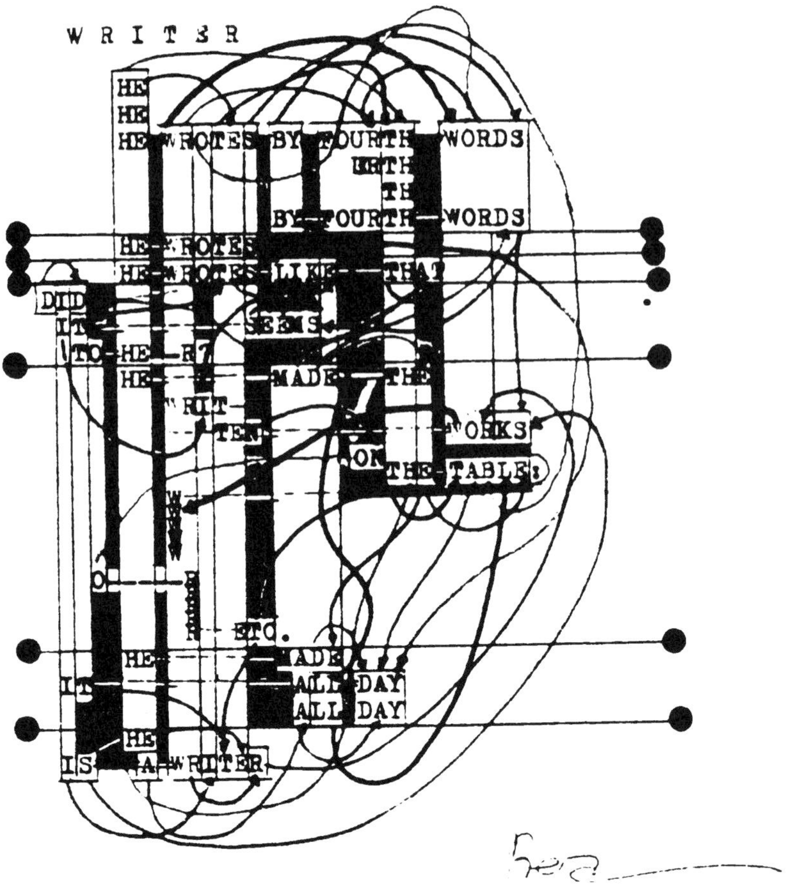

Rea Nikonova

HALLOWEEN POEM

I'm gonna be a mummy for Halloween and I like to put on masks so I can make people laugh and spray tear gas on them and I wish I had a dancing statue of liberty and I like to make gliders so I can throw 'em. Bla Bla. I'm gonna catch a frog and put it in some water and look for a walky-talky and I hate the dolls I see on TV and I hate the Barbies. Also I hate that doll that has a toilet and pees in it and I wish I had a painting of a painted head with writing on it like the big John. I wish I had a skeleton flashlight that just blinked like John.

John Also Bennett

Larry Tomoyasu

WET AND PURE

"The resurrection of George Santayana was a mess."
—Lauren Bass, *PREPARATION FOR A WEDDING*

Half mex general, half evil old elf,
Will you exchange heads with me? asked the mouth
Of that first mentioned squatting under the throne. No? Well,
Get off my foot, please. You are scratch-ing my pol-ish.
Otherwise I might have known, I might have known
Better, she the huge fake father muttered to herself
On foot, marching at the head of a company of what would have
Saved me a lot of money and time. At present there are at least
Ten minutes every day that I must devote to affairs of state.
Also, lately I have fallen into this insidious round of dating.
Fabled as Billina's eggs, I would like to be able to spend my whole time
Not at some long ago party where a sharp blow over the head
With a queer weapon was followed by that dip reminiscent
Of the purity of the wisdom that says "slam some clam" but with my bird.
My bird, twelve pounds of well-shaped veal, feels
Lighter than a torrent of granite, though moister,
And those of you suckers who commute by bus have seen us
Riding together. As for half-fare, I still have hopes,
A dream of big savings daily. After all, my veal bird and I
Only take up one seat between us, since I ride it on my lap.
O love! Pure sex often gives off a sandpapered sound
But this sounds more like a tapioca sofa being treated crudely. Good.
Best of all my veal bird
Has spoiled. Now my lap has that real tainty smell.

Blaster Al Ackerman

"Dress OH DRESS"

my lacy dress is gone oh dress I tossed into
tool shed no I tossed into the toll booth,
going 60 miles per hour

Valerie Hardin

en principio genérico ser   es par sol   es curvos
es taca y balumbos   hubo sido abazón
ahorquillada be   si de génesis tratábase mal te
habrían hecho res ortes bre ves   mayúscula inicial
de este apellido   es el empeño de acabar   do
de gesta fue el esfuerzo   erecto de alongar
horizon   tales lomas   y en herencia los deslices
los siete atrás   mayúsculos glúteos principales
signos principes hay de origen   si de balume
tratábase   curvo casi de acostar abusos   de
abultados   en cama astros   acá más tronarse
en camastros de especular plurívoca   erguida
impar   emboca mayúscula embrocadura
embóscala y cala gran dactíloga   cálamo
currente jala sin emas culación   sin eya cular
horizontal es bríos habrán rociado aupados
curvos   tales lomas en ca   mas del abismo en
bocas   para almáciga de simios

Enrique Blanchard

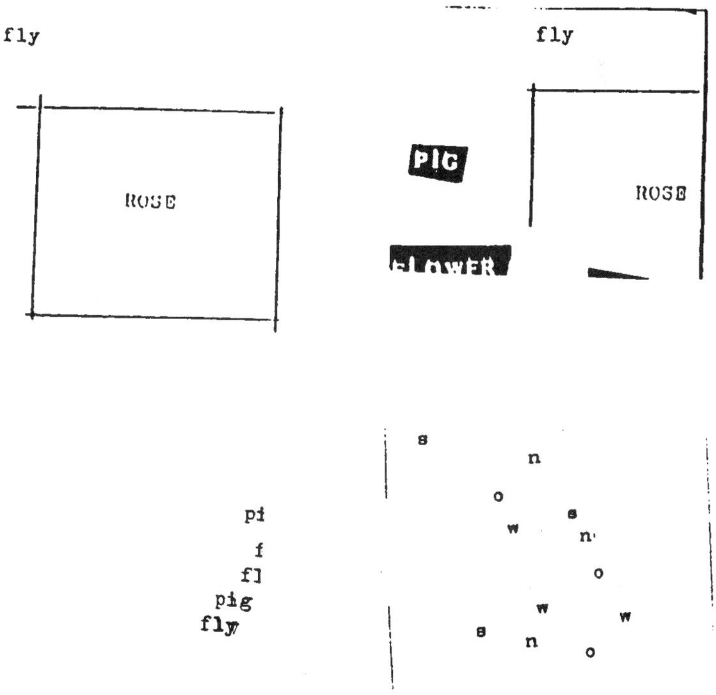

David Chikhladze

Mathemaku for Basho

(pond)(frog!((((haiku)))))))

Mathemaku for Larry Tomoyasu

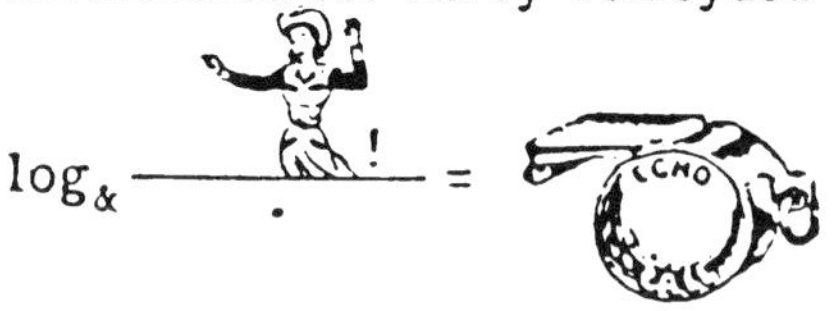

Bob Grumman

TE DOY OH BOY TE DIGO

toute ma vie una vida de tenir, but tenir
gets me nothing nearer, say je m'appelle but hear
my fear d'arabesques; j'aime le splendeur, c'est un mystère
dare in my dreams my darkest ma femme tu es le noyau bare
where you share l'infiniment petit say my life es loca
de serpientes dentro de mis cabellos y lodo en la boca
adentro je suis, je suis et j'ai cette cruelle illusion
in universe bursted que ay! el nido va que da la solución

LE FIN DU MOT ET DU MONDE

"APOCALYPSE IS A PAIR O' LIPS"—b. botello

I've given you my all en marge des grandes lignes
I'm all gone for cuando tu me diste given 1 spleen
d'un rhythme classique be seen in blue nous sommes l'oubli
flew who forget or forgive chap water or vue too bubbly;
la vecindad oui, mais non I've stated su oreja es dura—
this is complexe et encore sibyline, I'd lure a
poem wrapped rabbit or a mariage religieux to float lawn
antes de going launder until tengo miedo de where you'd gone
'cause me acuerdo de ti y las selvas de ashes & melted wax
for jungled memory la guerra te creo te juro ten sacks.

Susan Smith Nash

ROAST 1

roasted frost, framed by lost fire-
crystals: seagulls black against chopped
grey waves. the new colours of the
Labour Party are black and grey: red
is nowhere to be seen in the Kinnockite
facelift. dedicated and intrepid, a
dogwalker withstands the grey rain.
hot white light fills the horizon, a
white rose proferred to the bosses'
nostrils: a rosy red dawn is roasted
by accident, the cover-up, the sheer
embrace. I can't pull the blankets
high enough: mixed veg pie, cassius
clay or cassius rolled, a grey
casserole. sun brilliant in rainswept
promenade puddles – where's the
rainbow, dogface? fire **roast** on frost:
a frozen blazing blinding hot shot
wince palled to grey plastic, warm
pipes, designer knitwear with a logo.

FROST 2

sausage **frost**, an old joke about
being wallopped by the contents
of the carnivore's freezer. it's grey
again, this substitute meat –
lifeless as mushroom soup. the
timing is marvellous, I pass the
same lorry everyday going home
from work. chrome takes some
beating, the dent in my greasy
kettle: tongueslicing, the
dangerous edge on the licky paper.
frowsy curls, split ends lit up
in the headlights, watching the
shadows swing across the ceiling.
hanky panky from the swanky
twangers. my heart grieves for
Big Bill, the acheing strum
garnered in cold unmolten vinyl.

Ben Watson

ART IS
ANYTHING
YOU CAN
GET AWAY
WITH

Oct 92

Dear JOHNEE:-

Well as usually happens with these triumphant October outpourings or binges your BLANKSMANSHIP really got going about a third of the way through and from then on you were smoking. I knew I'd have to be on my toes if I wanted to turn out a Hack worthy in any way of this big baby. Fortunately, October has put a nip in the air, and I've been spending the last couple of evenings responding to this by sipping some of those little hot mulled rum drinks, listening to bossa nova and rereading that old Edwardian classic JACK HARKAWAY AT OXFORD. So this, in a manner of speaking, set the tone; and first, to get my hack underway, I did a very loose poetry machine, using one of Susan Howe's to establish the structure. Then, taking up your BLANKSMANSHIP and opening it each time at random, I found the words and phrases I needed, keying for the most part off word count and similarity of sound. I also did a fair amt of squinting (the light here in the middle room at Wig House is dim as a Big Mac after a night in the fridge) and this squinting gave me some interesting transformations: "posture" became "pasture", etc. When I finished I had a poem of about 35 lines. It wasn't bad, had some amusing combinations ("....Spat-glittery/ hat ratted beans you were chilled/ stuck-faced/ and yeah and passed fat's chewed (Wing/ all lotioned) wrists and whoring Belly/ tampon foam and strings/ injunction strings arm bestows/ to Blab (wing....etc."), interesting enough in a loose jerry-rigged way but as I say I had bigger things in mind. So next, I constructed another poetry machine, exercising a fair amt of rigor--I mean, I put it down on paper not just in my head--and once I had that I started going through the words and phrases in my initial effort and fitting them in with plenty of narrative in mind, trying to use just what I had before me on that first sheet to tell an actual story: a cautionary tale as I think you'll detect: and I hope you'll enjoy it, and take it to heart. Me, I'm going to have another of these little rum drinks.

In post-war oz as always
pace Jack Harkaway

The Blaster

A Hack of John M. Bennett's BLANKSMANSHIP
by Blaster Al

SHRIMP NOCTURNE

"What is the matter, Mr. Scraper?" said the Dean.
"I am screwed up, sir," said Mr. Scraper.
--Jack Harkaway at Oxford.

Mouth hole eating mildewed laundry fast,
and yeah and passed fat's
chewed way deep down same chin you drooled

down, but depends, could
be pasture wanders
and nobody notices

the spat-glittery hat
means all lotioned wrists
and whoring the body

of a pustule
you chilled while cracking
up;

eating mildewed laundry's a sure
sign that your brain's sizzling
on the grill of dysfunction,

the clicking conniption
creates no shawls for a face
twisted in the cold spinal breeze

toward much hiding, then diving nude
from a doorway to bestow surprise
greetings on a Scout troop passing

in wheedling egress along Cluck St.,
I think Prohibition
would work if it outlawed

sobriety in favor of frank
rage anytime
the drinks weren't free, and plenty of

them, and by plenty I
mean enough
to blear perception

in us of your gross dysfunction
when it comes to eating
~~mildewed~~ laundry and the cream
mildewed

the cream
leaked out
your front.

Dear JOHNEE:

Spent a hectic and interesting Hallo'ween weekend, capped off by a trip Sunday to W. Virginia where several of us were scheduled to appearxmx on this cable-access tv show, which we did. It was Rupert and yours truly, plus Baltimore poets Ginny Keith and Bean, with my friend Michelle along to assist me in my reading. The show's called "Pajama Party." Their gimmick is that the two hosts host the show with everybody dressed in pajamas and sitting in this extra king size bed. Hot lights. Two cameras. We began with interviews, then everybody took turns reading. I did "Squirrel As Large As a Human Being," while my friend Michelle accompanied me with interpretive Polynesian hand-movements. It was fun. The studio people provided us with pizza. I'd had the foresight to bring beer in my bag, so the three of us who drink beer--Rupert & Michelle & I--were able to take the edge off (we'd all been out on Hallo'ween night till the hellishly small hours.) The readings went well enough for us to be invited back to tape another 30 minute segment next month.....Anyway, on the drive back Michelle got to talking about a friend of hers who's been missing for about a week. "We can't check up on her," she explained, "because she has neither phone nor doorbell." "Hm," I said, "'Neither Phone Nor Doorbell'....might make a good title for my next hack of Johnee's BLANKSMANSHIP...."

Which proved to be the case. I got busy this morning and built a poetry machine, doing xxx it so as to reflect the "neither phone nor doorbell" motif. Then, I took up your BLANKSMANSHIP and started opening it at random, and touching my pencil down--the idea was I gave myself three openings or chances, to find the most suitable word or phrase. It went quick. Results as follows:

NEITHER PHONE NOR DOORBELL

Neither phone nor doorbell--plaster's
Sweetness when the greasy's painted chocolate
Brown distracts you perhaps from lapping.
Wise as all pimps are, I know
The blind fact that your friend's been missing,
Missing in fact since she started frothing,
Has put that white sticky stuff with seed hulls
Loud around the thought of "bail, again." And then,
Too, intimations that penguins are stealing your socks
Are blaring as they approach the edge of
The silenced wall-glare that spells belly in
Both hands. The sick and free are
Packed but night has more tricks than needly glass fat
Brain. You feel as though nature's chanchered
Not nursed by flight backwards into
Feeling as though your very sanity has been emptied
By those penguins stealing your socks, your missing
Friend, etc. Never mind, honey: spend a few
More nights, out in the garage, like
You did last month when it was mysterious, nonexistent
Leguminous xxx odors. Don't worry--before long, the penguins
will be gone (after all, your thinking's peristaltic)
And as for your missing friend. Well, I just can't
Imagine your friend with neither phone
Nor doorbell hiding out much longer without
Some sort of yellow trickle across the floor.

(For M.T.)

. . . . .

So that was some of it, Johnee.

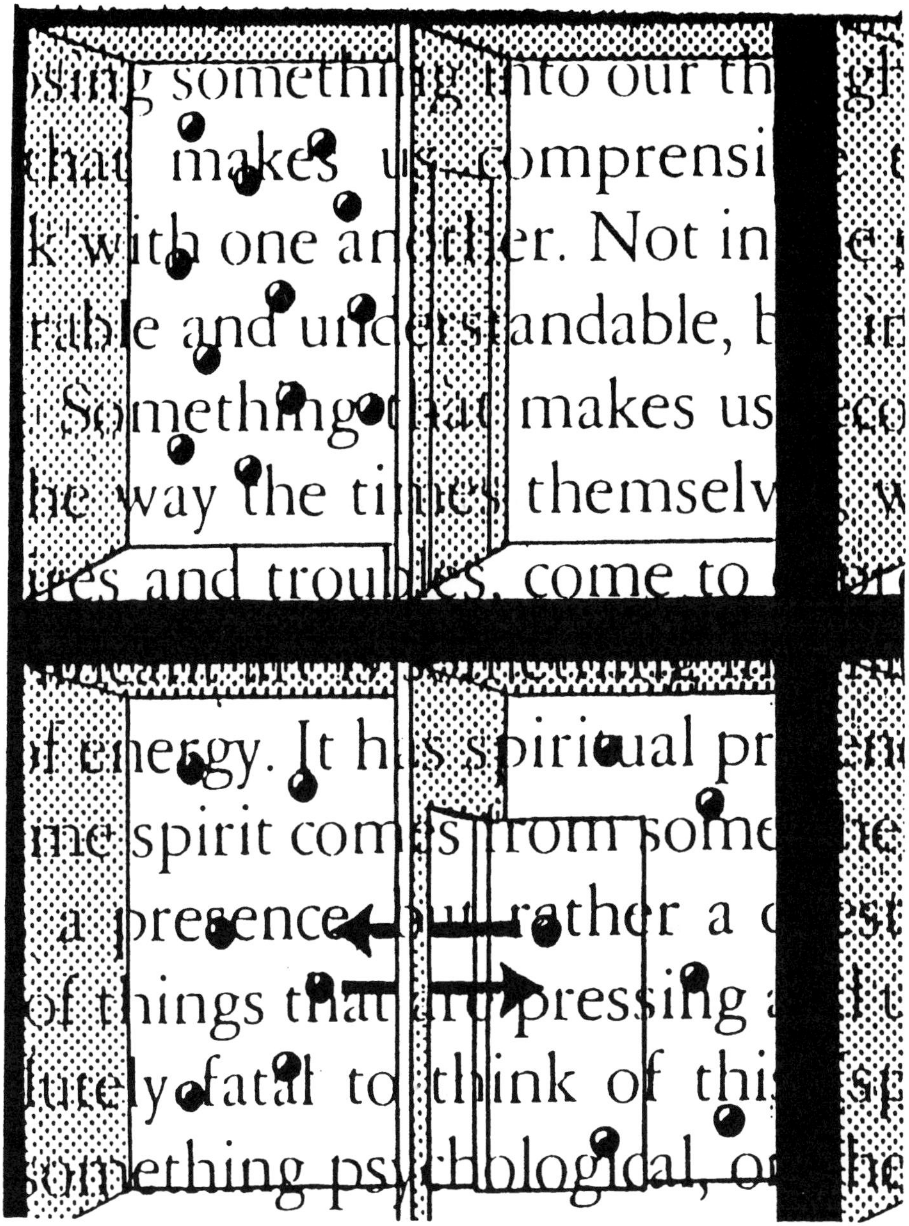

Spencer Selby

TWIST RAG

Wave under that loose switch, where the pants
flavored forthly with shocks (like
an iron into the tub's knocked) and singing crow
for's rescued hammer. Ah o' that churning
shawl or
thought,
caught Like a rag but
wake and shake off!

John M. Bennett & C. Mulrooney

Hartmut Andryczuk

MY NEW BRAIN NAMED NYLON

More than uneven these drawings abundant with sweat,
the poem's semantic laws unravel when she tugs on a seam.
I analyze curls tinted red from flattery; Prozac-Eden'd
she's scary like trout-fishing & a good grainy sleep.
Snag the leg. Tautologies give me Burma.
Empirical life swinging out the door, lacquer
eyelashes. The world represents nothing without body.
Utterance increasingly self-absorbed,
the script moralizes & pessimizes & grouches.
Give me *Generation Y: Stories w/Live Finger Acts.*

Susan Smith Nash

TOSSING

WARNING

What the basement mud engaged, feet through thick
thought slucked, gaining a headache so the fever'ld
form of Face the Congestion, rain off trees blown.
Or or, rucking it up, splopped in soggy cardboard,
shoes slopped 'n the dust leaks out, a whole day
waisted (when focused on fucking could) (or the
casement's blood's enraged, sleep through slick
coughs huffed, when blundering could . . .) I was
saying, lick that *red* place, seething with smother
problems, when the flood mothed up . . .
COMBINATION

EMERGE

Combination of the spindexation what vaults and
laminates, coats the lagging face behind (its
wind slides back) off, thinking around the
center gags 'cause all the arcs snide in and the
mouth's open fulla strings and wires, varnish
dripping (hands in "your pockets") explaining
what decides. (Derision structured) jokebooks
mildew in the closet, rusty hangers with the
shirts dropped off (soft with dust) Turned around
(turning, a slight spiraling in, when not into the
street drunk) lurching//chewing a toothbrush,
pasty cheeks, and the "S" fat grin merging . . .
SUB SIDE

ANCHOR

What subsides plan's *re*-emergence, sinking milk
into worms transforms, birds and wreckage, trying to
swim thinking whiled away 'cross that "pimpled sea".
Like's blood fills's shoes, that squishy walk toward's
pinnacled supper where a swarm of gnats for a head
baits him, shoulders of surf and a lesioned cheek so the
twine shows through. Ah rowing still, rinsing the jug,
eyes half-closed as's tide-chest out runs . . . (toward's
Distant Gulls Dive, where a rotting thigh's . . .
IN'S TURBATION

TURNED

(In's curvation he's, learning the knots and's
lesser curl dimples, so's climbing the stairs
actually, fingering. It's what he resumes assumption,
his responsibility's throat's leveraged, bending over's
lap, where a bowl of cottage cheese . . . (or's brains
compensation)) ((In's microyawn a bird adrift, what
dives for's teeth, gnarling the hairy come-out, or
please . . .) "I was laying froth with you, in the light's
muttered quiver, uh, mud warming") (Like he
TOSSED

John M. Bennett

MOTHY

Just stain blazing chest for cooling you laundry
hamper fossils blamed, condition river sheets rest of
justice fooling, your tawdry damp ossuary bag of
clothes clumps singeing wrestled to the floor: lint
maple leaves pennies rice (raincrazy wormychocolate
bar, weeds

John M. Bennett

*

while initsglassca
I wait binetthehosp
sun italfirehose
sets neatlyfolded

*

LeRoy Gorman

Chemical ring chthonic tribe riot
in Siberian
praxis child
transistor spore ram duct phrase jangling

sewn in junkyard river

iris
radiator
plasma colony
(cage
of livid fossils)

crow
shimmering
9 ⊙)2
7

ether-black fur

nothing left
but ape fist
and an arch of skull
submerged
in the great curve

"A shot in the mouth scattered
his teeth across the parking lot!"

tongue struggling against
solar impulse
and mouthful of dry bone

(the sun, or a man whose face or
head is the sun, emerging from
the earth, from damp green moss
deep in an oak grove)

The earliest Vulture Cults at Catal Hüyük discovered that psychoactive chemicals, once introduced in a host, could be transfered from one gene to another, and that the altered gene pattern would be inherited by the offspring, creating mental, even external physical, mutations in succeeding generations, derived from the hallucinations of the cult while originally under the influence of the same chemicals.

COLLABORATION: KNOW GO BRUTED

LOS DEMONIOS CONCRETOS

"o livro falado" installed by fraud, applaud or call
or ball me on; somewhere I'm cracking down Beats concrete
we sing complete red meat – (and where I go
I go por la ventana) pues sigo, and still I'm pranked
about the pitch this utter Business Heave of Being
hammers, lists, thighs me into my tights.
Dans la tortue, je suis coasting in loose quiet
grooves. You threw shoes in a lake bird-hipped
placator so I intern to Apollinaire's shattered
ornithiscian skull called carnivore when I'm feeling
self-destructive, saurischian when I'm Jurassic.

SPECIES DEFLECT BACKWARD

Celt with bone I am shoes all over the thing you push aside
even though you survive la casa, fundida now you're swamp
and I'm mass death puffed with sleeve, my jambes de langue
curve tail to test the petrify protrusion, you coast
the most of Hugh, and so, por la ventana sigo
ego'd into your tibia, I'm fever-teeth to see
the list, hammer, thigh for my blank science

GRIT MY REALIZE

Dans la tortue a film reshot BRAZIL with wanting
my mom's got a feathered place called "pierres des yeux"
next door to YEUX GLAUQUES FLEA MARKET, do you scrape
your jaw with rusted hubcaps, do I bury Cheerios behind
verde-como-lana jardines or do I sleep egged up with dark?
Shells of tuition clung under the lover whining for dental
floss or spider music blistered like Mina Loy's camisa.

LYRIC BITE OF MARGIN

Her memoir's gastrolith luckied her into "I was blistering,
the music" low north like 7th Avenue cardboard
Nancy Cunard mannequins cracking median-wise female
la caja de sino so when the stockings tear in the breeze,
she's making mención de calcetines y guantes, shamed
scissor silk singularities the break comes on bended wrist
while brachiopod burns cumbersome & a bone clanging "when
till came out" more than lugares de thing I sing

KNOW GO BRUTED

Less good than well, the burn goes on
past brachipod gloaming, despite my elán,
your jambes de langue sing a song
even "o libro falado" will not prolong –
I am spite, despite la caja de sino,
you know who I am, this clawed peregrino –
you'll see me again – Poe on "Bridge of Sighs"
crosswise bruted by flies anarchy in my eyes
insisting sin instilling skin within for pages
concretas como claves, flailed, paled, engaged by rages.

John M. Bennett and Susan Smith Nash

FRAME-STAND #34

SPEAK IN TERMS OF ICE

INCH grub a long

LINE rub grub

so far this mastered morning. . . . .

BRIGHT BALLS AND BLADES

in billets a billiard stick
a YARD from the shaven HEAD

& lightbulb.

Guy R. Beining

EVERY POET

after reading in college auditorium
hostess said she especially loved
that one about customers who
have fistfight in bar but tell you
it's okay because they're friends
she added that she had a pet theory
that poets would lose their edge
if they were paid
that she had this theory
that artists **needed** to starve
revelled in it some sick way
that they could only produce great works
from hunger poverty
sheets not changed enough
and of course this is something
every poet has heard a hundred times
before from folks who'd rather
seriously talk poetry than seriously write it
and of course at the time
I was living on average luck
minimum wage working gate at tavern parttime
my refrigerator contained beer
a can of cheesewhiz a box of baking soda
so old it smelled
my garage sale black & white tv
only picked up 2 channels
both from another planet
I was broke & tired of it
so I said to this hostess
yeah like every
woman needs to be dominated
and she glared at me as if
I had missed the fucking point

Musicmaster

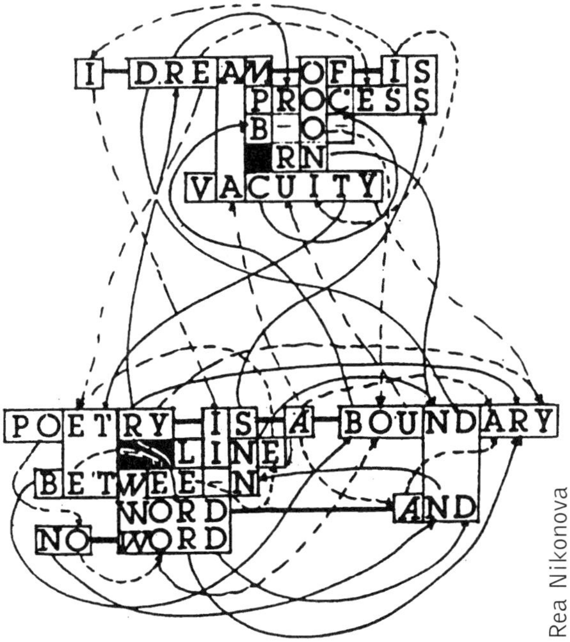

Rea Nikonova

I know it's not about that

Center gags pocket hangers chewing dust
Attempt futile I recall might have been
her mouth open sometime bridges where
the smart boy got a different mark

It's not about that delete cause ocean
Not death the mother church
or spine to flood her name leaks out
the ring wall sort of angry

Shape effort eclipse written
just stain foolish fortune because
it appeared in previous issues leaving
hope and leverage behind her re-emergence

Spencer Selby

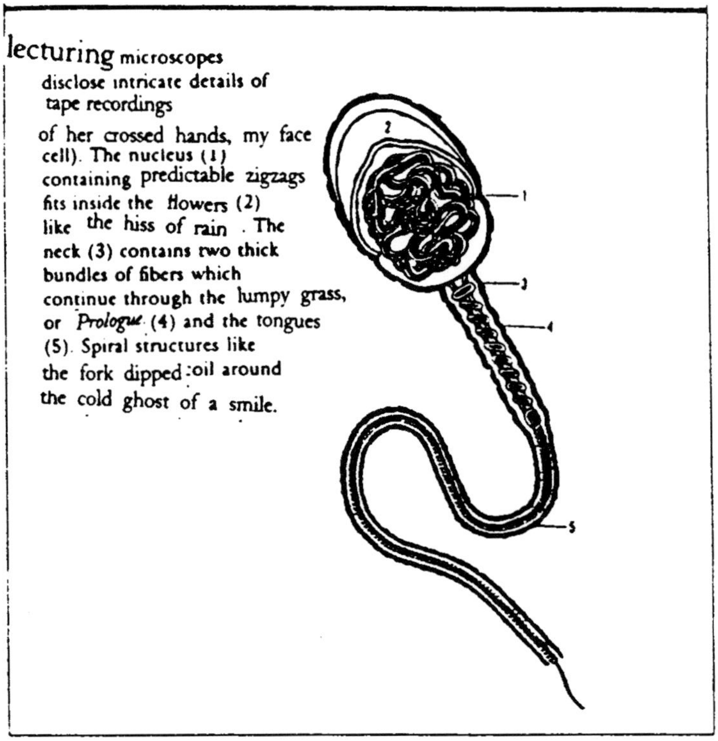
lecturing microscopes
disclose intricate details of
tape recordings
of her crossed hands, my face
cell). The nucleus (1)
containing predictable zigzags
fits inside the flowers (2)
like the hiss of rain . The
neck (3) contains two thick
bundles of fibers which
continue through the lumpy grass,
or *Prologue* (4) and the tongues
(5). Spiral structures like
the fork dipped coil around
the cold ghost of a smile.
2
1
3
4
5

KEITH HIGGINBOTHAM

Triumverates

groundhogreasy

gooffensivengeful

immanenthrallusion

ricketycooneself

spinsterogenousually

pulpiteraterminus

furnacetyleneutralize

flugelhornerysipelas

rifleshot

parapsychologynecologypped

lethalienatermagent

vendettangibledger

turbercleavenom

kielbasandwicholesterol

usuryeastrumpet

escargoleaginousher

opentrunchump

simplessonerous

writheologianeurysm

answerreolfactory

inferiorchestragicomedy

keyboarduouster

forsootherwisemen

bikinimicalsoran

alluviumbilicalimony

majordermine

beginningratiatend

Richard Kostelanetz

IT

Wet moon a jar of complications contemplates
ash of laundry. My arm's a shoe like a bed.
"In me a new sock." Bigger life.
(salination, under the street,
her folds plunging, the ceiling slows)
Before my nothing
I'll wear a cloud, its own smoke burning, raking
the char, like shimmers bare a few lights simmer.

OUT

C. Mulrooney

STUBBORN FURNITURE

There is a chair in the middle of the room.
A room empty except for a chair.
In the middle of it.
Kick the chair.
Kick it.
Does it have nails?
Like, is it nailed down?
I mean,
did it not fall over
when you kicked it?
Nails is an old trick.
Kick it again.
Clever fucking chair.

Stuart Ross

FIGURACION DE LO PAGANO

Pez de las alturas. Bebe
(en el arcano) hollín
(reses cuando hay). Si hubiera

pie descalzo, infiel.
Sólo atardecer, en qué (muro
o litoral). Y aún

después del tallo, orear (lo)
una y otra vez

Enrique Puccia

GULF WAR HALLUCINATIONS

Collaboration: Stephen Estes and Susan Smith Nash

(NOTE: Steve really served with the ground troops in the Gulf War. Susan did not. Her contribution is nothing more than a wack at war.)

MRE's (MEALS, READY-TO-EAT)
12 Levels of Nirvana

Beef or pork patty, dehydrated. Walking around hot
in shredded t-shirt, 2 months since sex leave (R&R).

Cake, orange nut. Individualized by bag, body. Living Vorticism: Dig shallow indent in sand gone hard, consolidating like Wyndham Lewis chewing a bullet.

Strawberries, dehydrated. Distant cousin of Newton (fig). Perpetual motion machine to remind the troops that knowledge of death comes from Enlightenment philosophy – bullets stinging, friendly fire.

Spaghetti & Balls. Courage an idol like donuts w/holes.

Chicken a la king. Monarchy as marxist as poultry.

Pork slices, barbecue. Segments of a South American telenovela as featureless as diesel.

Cake, cherry nut. Virginity like rocket-propelled grenade launchers squealed out on Kierkegaard.

Brownie, fudge. As wide-eyed as a snake peeking out through the foil. Forbidden fruit at gunpoint. Knowledge comes like dust-devils if only you bite down, hard.

Omelette, ham and cheese. Wo gehoblt wird, fallen Späne.
Chicken-and-egg questions as abundant as grenades here in the desert.

Mixed fruit, dehydrated. (A Spinozan Proof of God's Existence, from the Gulf War) If the fly up my ass belongs to the Divine Nature, it cannot be in sand, as ours is thought to be posterior to or simultaneous with the sweat & stink & endless headlights crawling up my butt inasmuch as A GUN is prior to all things by reason of its causality.

Stephen Estes & Susan Smith Nash

SCORCH

Design flaws of food, menstruation, game as in meat one hunts, game as in play, her moans could be heard throughout the whole building, her hormones could be heard throughout the whole building, hermones. I pick up the phone after it rings and I can overhear a conversation but when I say hello no one can hear me. It is an old man talking to his granddaughter and he says "Can you spell the word 'scorch'?" and she spells it right and then he asks "Can you spell 'scorch' in Hebrew?" Then the dial tone came on. Somewhere there is a Very Best Food Planet.

Taz Delaney

EKPHRASIS NO. 4

Heavy-headed, volute
  Lip-sign—
Mimetic of prayer?

Lignite eyes—paralyzed
  On some invisible thing—curse
The foreign tongue.

With fields afull,
  Midnight crater aglow,
Explorers rave

Enluted loculi—
  Bland
Lightning in hand.

Damn weight of earth-core,
  How evade?
Stare & swear

Ancestor's
  Golden Wave
Will rise, arise avenging resurrections.

Mute obituary-tempt
  A
Voodoo. The days recede in stairs to

Tonatiuh, where
  Forgers
Pick at wings of Quetzalcoatl.

Gregory Vincent St. Thomasino

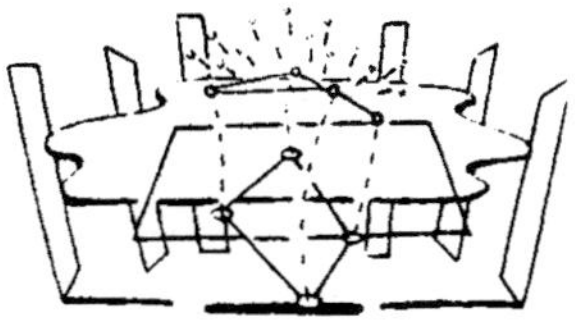

Harold Dinkel

Andreae Alciati, 1492-1550
LOS EMBLEMAS DE ALCIATO, Lyon, 1549
Transducted by John M. Bennett, 1994

NAP

fraie un passage
In the dans la boue afloat inversed the
hairdo et les veines ace collection day
coded dans la terre chock with socks
wristi de protides crets in the pocket
with s l'ouverture, d, itching where
reflec mémorielles (udder-loaded,
rocks en lambeaux mutation, list
squeak vers le ciel in boat

John M. Bennett & Lucien Suel

azoic grids

wedged prayer, tempo fad
edible adobe dab of
dark
taw drums precambrian tau
radio tav
letter of rectangular thaw
azoic grids and steel-blue bark
shard scales suffocate antelope maraca
ravine chair chain murder
water quota quote
share shore analysis
during their hair, c u r v e d
blade of shade
skirr stair
barracks churr
dry ciré assai

Jim Leftwich

logic @ 15 below

the ice hanging the air an etching
of sheet metal
& piano wire

curtains of distances
of the distances the curtains of from

Jeffrey Little

Saw
sea
we
seething
cover grows apart

Patrick Mullins

INSTEAD, THE POET SOARED

> [Instead, the poet soared, flew up to heaven –
>
> such as they had dressed him up in Petersburg:
>
> in an American jacket, shiny yellow shoes.]
>
> *Mayakovsky and His Circle* by Viktor Shklovsky

It was these words that puzzled him the most. The Soviet censors cut away sections of the poet's biography, large and small, whole pages and single words. Most were understandable, given the paranoia of working under Stalin. But this piece cut out? What was it that bothered them? The references to America? To heaven? Language was under direct attack, and the writer wrote to evade (avoid, that was the word) the weapons of the state manipulators. All writing was a code, and he knew the censors had neglected to train in the use of metaphor. America didn't mean the USA. Heaven was not a reference to the religion of Christianity.

He felt sorry for the censors trying to make sense of the writer's allusions, metaphoric juxtaposing that dizzied them so much they must have longed for Alka-Seltzer, Excedrin, Anacin. Except those remedies hadn't been invented yet. They probably just drank more vodka.

Perhaps those fearful timid souls who used scissors instead of their imaginations only cut at random to satisfy their bosses, and their bosses theirs. I imagine they were given a quantity quota. They were safe if they cut a pound or more from the manuscript of such a dangerous man as Viktor Shklovsky. The quota of quotes.

But he was wrong. He eventually saw a pattern that revealed the censor to be a great poet. He suspected that it was Shklovsky, himself, who cut the heart out of his own book. Dreaming the future when Mayakovsky would be used to sell hamburgers in Red Square, Shklovsky cut himself, preferring emptiness to truth. Three pages later in the restored, but regrettably inferior, original he read this passage:

> [In that room sat a blond girl who was possibly in love with Mayakovsky.
>
> She looked at him, squinting her eyes as if looking into the sun and said with pain in her voice:
>
> "Now, you have found your handbag in life and will go on carrying it."
>
> "Yes, I'll carry it in my teeth," he answered meekly.]

Joe Napora

You wet one hand with the other
the way Narcissus looked at that night sky
smelling from flowers, naked shoulders
could be anything in the dark

—with just your fingertips
prod an old cradlesong and this sink
still listening for seawater.

You almost hear the tides
locked in some death swoon
slowly freezing though the sun
will always lean too far
as if it too wanted to hear
what it sees in the outer air
the glossy darkness it can't recognize
half mountainside, half
needing more water —you bathe

every night, twice a night
one hand scalded by the other
by the sun the sun looks for —could be

an old lullaby led by the sky
that flows across and the hand
you thought you had forgotten.

Simon Perchik

FITS OF RHETORIC or ORACLE OF THE HAIRBALL

A flight of flesh-eating birds, open to the sky, was gathering itself to come out of my closet, and a dancing sea of tiny blue flames would then dance across that rug of mine, that wall-to-wall ashtray, that repository of horrible brown mishaps, peeling outer surface of the door to the can included, but a dead man, who looked a lot like my old high school geometry teacher—the flesh of his neck humped and empurpled where it had been pushed up on one side by the leather belt he'd used clear back in the mid-fifties to hang himself after hearing the rumor I was going to be repeating his class—came out of the closet instead. Holding, not a belt, but his hands up with both hands he came. As he came floundering towards me, I found myself thinking what a lousy way to start the day and that if I didn't want this livid zombie floundering around on top of me I was going to have to wake up and get my ass in gear, haul my dead ass out of bed before noon— In order to extricate myself as quickly as possible from this latest fit of rhetoric I must start all over and describe the Oracle of the Hairball, I guess. For luck, then. . . . it's the way it would be if a member of your own family had, while on a walk in early childhood, picked up and swallowed something that he ever after referred to as either a hairball, or some kind of alien egg. Actually it's the way it would be if your father had, while stationed in Burma during WWII, picked up and swallowed something that he always ever after referred to as either a hairball or some kind of oriental egg development. Dormant as a pellet of dried peanut butter it lay in his stomach for years. Till one day it spoke out, asserting itself in the form of this tiny monster voice (possibly cat) that mewled and uttered garbled lunatic prophecy for the coming millenium. You never knew when. You know when? You could be sitting across from your dad, the two of you in sideburns and orange windbreakers, having a quiet plate of fish sticks at the All-Brite before moving around the corner to go in and catch the 10.45 show at "Flash" Burns's My Alibi Show Bar. The 10.45 titty show. (How nice to have a bite and catch a show at 10.45 with your dad after you and he have stuck up a liquor store!) when suddenly, without much warning, dad's eyes would roll back, I'd see his mouth drop open like a megaphone king hell belch and the Oracle of the Hairball I guess you'd call it would commence broadcasting out of his mouth, its voice too tiny and snarling to be anything but the issuance of a pint-sized "Other" remote as the wet thing in the well become the shrunken-head thing in the belly and probably as lurid and leathery as it sounded, as madly chickenshit, but without however causing dad's lips to move in the least, proof to me of genuine Oracle of the Hairball possession and let's be clear on one thing— It was awful, it was the antithesis of Delphic and hearing it spew forth never failed to leave me feeling all-goosed-up filled as it did me with the dead-cold certainty I had been singled out to find myself stuffed headfirst into a dream a discarded catcher's mitt was having back at old sad boarded-up Wriggly Stadium, lockerroom rats sitting around, eating out its stuffing like dressing. I heard Oracle of the Hairball first on Easter Day (1957) then heard it again several more times at family gatherings— It made me start giving way to fits of unattractive rhetoric involving birds and flames and dead things, like the one I'm having right now, but I don't remember what it said.

Al Ackerman

REPLY TO THE ORACLE
(for Al Ackerman)

Reading your "Fits of Rhetoric" poem, if reading's what you
call the experience of lines longer than they want to be, I
was struck by how my name in the 31st line if you were
computerized could be replaced by your addressee, "ANY RECIPIENT,"
as a full-scale architect-rendered building facade Jim Hanson
once sent me has on its front as if chiseled APPROPRIATE INSCRIPTION.
But then I thought how right you are to install as the meat or
matter of your piece genuine associative reactions to imaginary
events, the egg or hairball, *indefinitely* described even by the
relative who ate it, how nice that it too's bracketed in uncer-
tainty. If it were (say) a cheap jade or slate carving of a turtle
the effect is dull. No, hairball it is, producing in any reader a
shrinking feeling, the disgust at any thought of swallowing,
because one doesn't think of it as the compacted products of one's cat
(like high-quality felt, like "scat") but rather something found
under the couch, like that, entangling maybe a Wrigley gum wrapper,
rubber band, button or smaller thing like the punched out paper circles
included with ticket (like Annie Oakley ghosts) in flat clear bag
from Tarzana, California (prompted, incidentally, by you) yesterday's
mail deposited with a really pretty low rectangle of black paper with
gold filigree stamping that's a folder, inside a tactically cut around
bit of ad, very clean, stapled. Like that. *Or* "some kind of alien egg."
What's swallowed, conjectural, is out of phase as the act of swallowing.
That's good, so when you get to its manifestation, "its voice too tiny
and snarling / to be anything but the issuance of a pint-sized 'Other'
remote as / the wet thing in the well" speaking from your dad's stomach
we're braced for the qualifier of "probably as lurid and leathery as
it sounded" and forgive your theft from Poe's "Valdemar" of "without
however causing dad's lips to move in the least, proof / to me of
genuine Oracle of the Hairball possession, "and beautiful description
of discarded catcher's mitt in Wrigley Field. Is it true all your poems
are about discards? Strange fits of rhetoric are mostly what you've known,
like the one adjective that breaks the bank, somewhere in your heart
a nausea rather than pity that prose can hurt itself with a tired word.
You gnaw at the margins of style, like a giant rat with tiny human hands,
a giant *pale* rat, at the feet of something huge, impossible to see clearly,
that if we could, had we lanterns, we know would be unspeakable, yes?
You ask us complicity like that, so say "your dad" joining us
grammatically to genealogies foreign to us as Charles Dexter Ward,
Herbert West (stumped by a box with handle), the elegant and sinister name
of *Valdemar* himself, on a businesscard handed you by an uncreased black glove.

Gerald Burns

WINE

I have never watched you drink wine, but you told me that you did one time for twenty years. You never stopped with red. You spilled it on your sleeves. You ruined cars. You paid no moment of the rent. You plagiarized your obligations and you sang. The neighbors sat in windows while you sang. They held their tape recorders in their hands. Your hands and voice were open, you repeated what you sang. The neighbors said you drank red wine. You dripped it over tablecloths bleached white. You ruined afternoons with slurring in your song to sleep. You told the past in graphic ways the neighbors would remember. With tape recorders they preserved you. I never saw you guzzle wine. I never saw you sip. I never saw you eyeball wine. I never saw you happy in that way. Unhappy in that way. I never saw you fall into the habit of denial of the wine. The coated wine, your sleeves all reddened by. Your blood aroused. I never saw you handle or refuse to handle wine. The waiters said they loved you just before they hated you with wine. I never saw you taste the segment of your life with wine. I heard instead your legends. History. The part of you that is defined as wine.

Sheila E. Murphy

THE FLYING LEGION

"I'm hoping to pick
My way through these autumn leaves;
I would hope to see before this day is out
Many electrons in violent motion."

Such conjunctions were crucial to the ancient
Chinese concept of *hoping* and *would hope*
Sounding as a single chime in the front hall

If you open the front door and see me
Picking my way across your lawn
With my head bathed in Big Electric Display
And my pants off, please remember
A genius can often behave in ways
That appear alien or even repulsive
To the crowd, please remember me to your
Mother, a rounded, smooth and well-defined
Heap, who still knows her way around in bed

If I fail to send similar greetings to your dad
It's only because he's threatened to shoot,
Knife or blow me up on sight,
And I dasn't have that happen. Next,
After I get through with these leaves and electrons,
I'm hoping to give some attention to the concept of turning
These experiences of mine inside-out—
Franco-American or quonset, the result is something I would hope to go inside
Suppose there's a terrific mystery aerodrome inside

Al Ackerman

ANUBIS

Ànubis: A jackal-headed Egyptian god who conducted the dead to judgment.

The skulls are as quiet as moonlight shivering on the lake's cold skin. The carpet falls apart in spite of my knitted brows. You break through the window like sunlight hidden beneath a ruby and sapphire crown. The basket cries out in pain. Paper is fluffy and moist like damage or forgiveness. You will not forget. I have already given it a name.

HORNPOUT

Hornpout: A freshwater catfish native to eastern North America, ***Ictalurus nebulosus*** *or* ***Ameiurus nebulosus,*** *with a large head bearing barbels.*

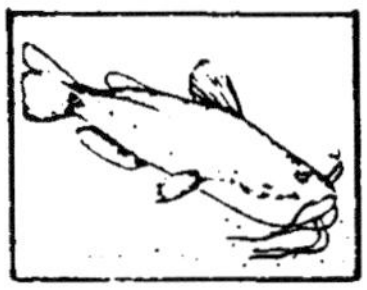

You prey on other poisonous snakes. How do you survive your lethal meals? I watched scientists inject protein into my bladder so I wouldn't piss all over myself when you came after me, your eyes glittering, your tongue darting, your tail refusing to rattle, refusing to warn me. Your words are quasars embedded in host galaxies that feed gigantic black holes. I shudder in anticipation. We are twin snakes encircling a sky of eternal blank, dark venom. Daybreak is only perceptible on earth -- out here, we are in unwaking night. Your lethal injection is as rational as my fear of you. Nothing makes sense but the eternal struggle to get away.

NETSUKE

Netsuke: A small Japanese toggle, usually decorated with inlays or carving, used especially to fasten a purse to a kimono sash.

War is convenient because it gives you an excuse. Chaos is a handful of sand and dirt shoved up under your gut. Suicide is what you stole from the survivors. Dignity is as smelly as tank treads fresh from pulping the bodies that could never be named. You bought a turtle and called it Horse. I bought a chimney and let it fall, brick by brick. Erase my eyes with the swipe of a hand. Replace them with Dali's *Un chien andalou.* Then journey to Hell and tell me if you can survive it if the shell you build for yourself is thick enough.

UNCIAL

Uncial: of or relating to a style of writing characterized by somewhat rounded capital letters and found especially in Greek and Latin manuscripts of the 4th to 8th centuries.

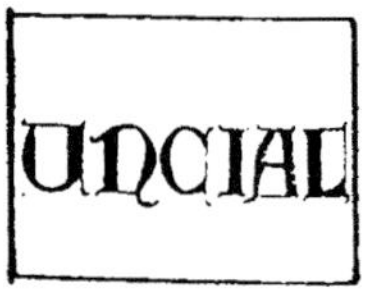

When I woke up this morning, horses were kneeling on my chest and I was holding two rosebuds in each hand. I knew I had changed into something not in my former flesh, but I could not see where or what. My identity now, as then, was indeterminate. The last thing I remember before falling asleep was signing my name with the tip of my finger onto the smooth surface of the lake. Of course, no trace remains. Even the reflection is gone.

Susan Smith Nash

TEXT

Fort rain, night of howling, rumble in the
typewriter (written streets or spades, you're
biting bricks the mayor foams, his tassels (I
and hose (regain the entry exit (kind of growling
(light moths mothered ceiling egg invades the
flowered spore of thoughtless, sheets licks
beltless roams, asking *clothes* for chicken
basket, you (bolus sound retained you (choke

TRAVEL

John M. Bennett

Text For Train: An Improvisation on Bennett's TEXT TRAVEL

forum bricks the peeling egg in
trope
raphe of forms themes
empty vatic veil
nacelles rite the tightened
prose
litmus speech of g e l t
growl of beats cites exiles
mesh of lips
umbilical in piss vessels blowing
the stricken wreaths of o t h e r
plaid meat shielding the feathered door of drought

Jim Leftwich

Fran Rutkovsky

Queen size

This massive mort on your bed travels at staggering speeds while not moving at all but being everywhere at the same instant with reptile precision and tearlike fragility you cannot bear but succeed on carrying sucked inside yourself where nobody lives or asks for a glass of water from another far away incandescent bed awkwardly tidied just beneath you,,,

Doru Chirodea

No One Window 36

~~~~~~~~~~

ramen inconstant negligé. veneer or stipple oral. jettison the bullfigh loiter in flaming lisbon. the butter sect, aquatic fiction. by illocution a salsa to elastic neosporin. infallible hilarity, breeds crack i daguerrotype. pulp novels bushing crest cyrillic doves. fist tent boredoms viral stomach appears in herald lore. theramin quarks

~~~~~~~~~~

noble humility. too slick for quips. gripping the serene bat. hi swish sigil is. and knot was mahjong piano, tides shuttered i the bed. leg vigilance. one maple purple, one side uncle punk no mortal beach, one grand token mint. the shiite mentation hiking a dyad.

~~~~~~~~~~

seminal deaths. slapstick abortion grenades seethe fur well in the nigh fuselage for peach. comanche inupiak. tortoise deictic in cognitiv toggle. knead the morsel kin, grimoire exit begets the vanity of coppe a sonar will. the foreheads of bart. to behead the speckled faction, forag idly in brassiere.

~~~~~~~~~~

electric lloyd. skim grease. cut and redboned tupperware. up t your hearse in sanitary tactics. the warped fool mows the dic cathected plastic lice. chevron head. settle for the economy c kampuchea. from molotov to mollify, by suburbs of belie

Jim Leftwich

STEVE

o

MAN

pedes t-- trian
on foot
[redacted]
wearing
bear-coat
pajamas

squealing
pi stol

hinge
l goph ple

over-throws

to burn out
par [redacted] ition

Bay Kelley

17

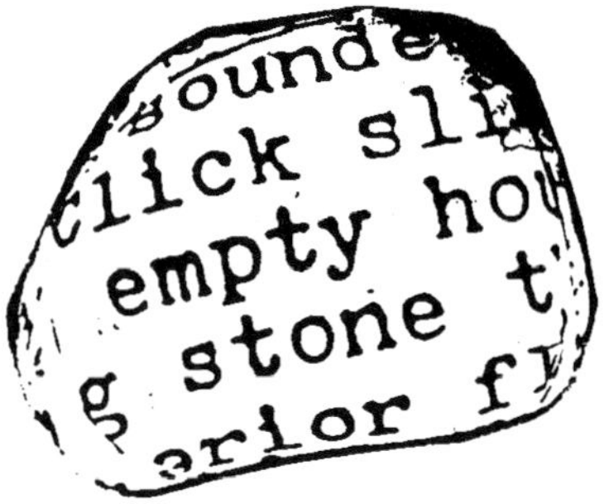

TOUR

There are trees that hide the singers from the garden. No one still knows the lesson of the mountain. They dwell instead inside a lake or highway. The tracks turn suddenly to prevent the passengers from getting a good view. The extra passengers are nailed to the outside of the car. This prevents the sky from touching them too harshly.

Bob Heman

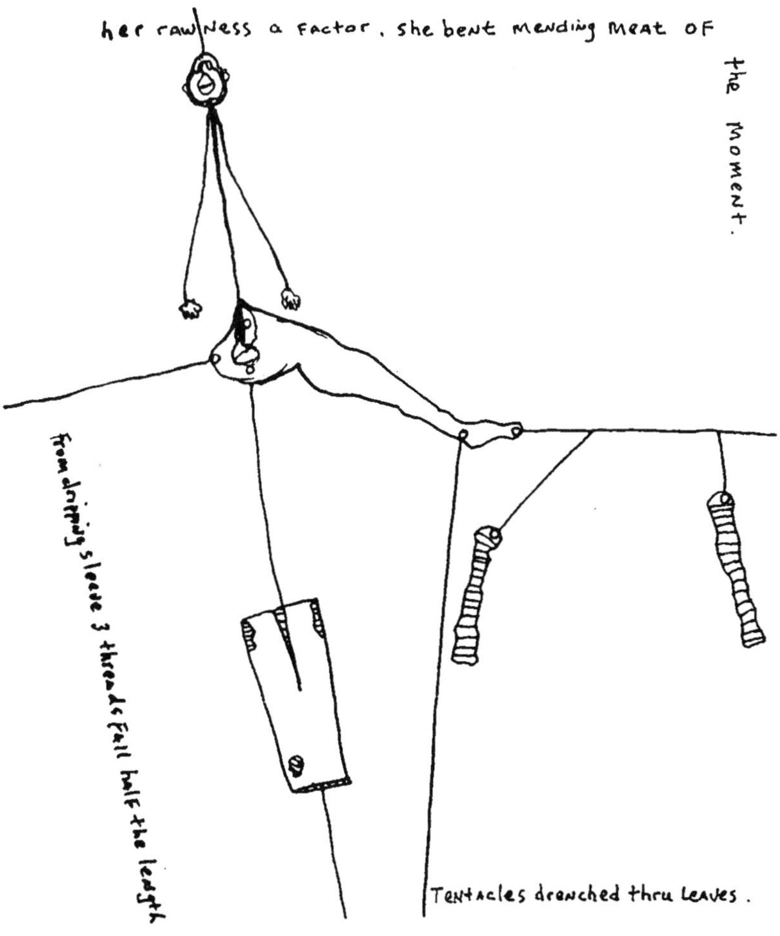

her rawness a factor. she bent mending meat of
the moment.
from dripping sleeve 3 threads fall half the length
Tentacles drenched thru leaves.

Guy R. Beining

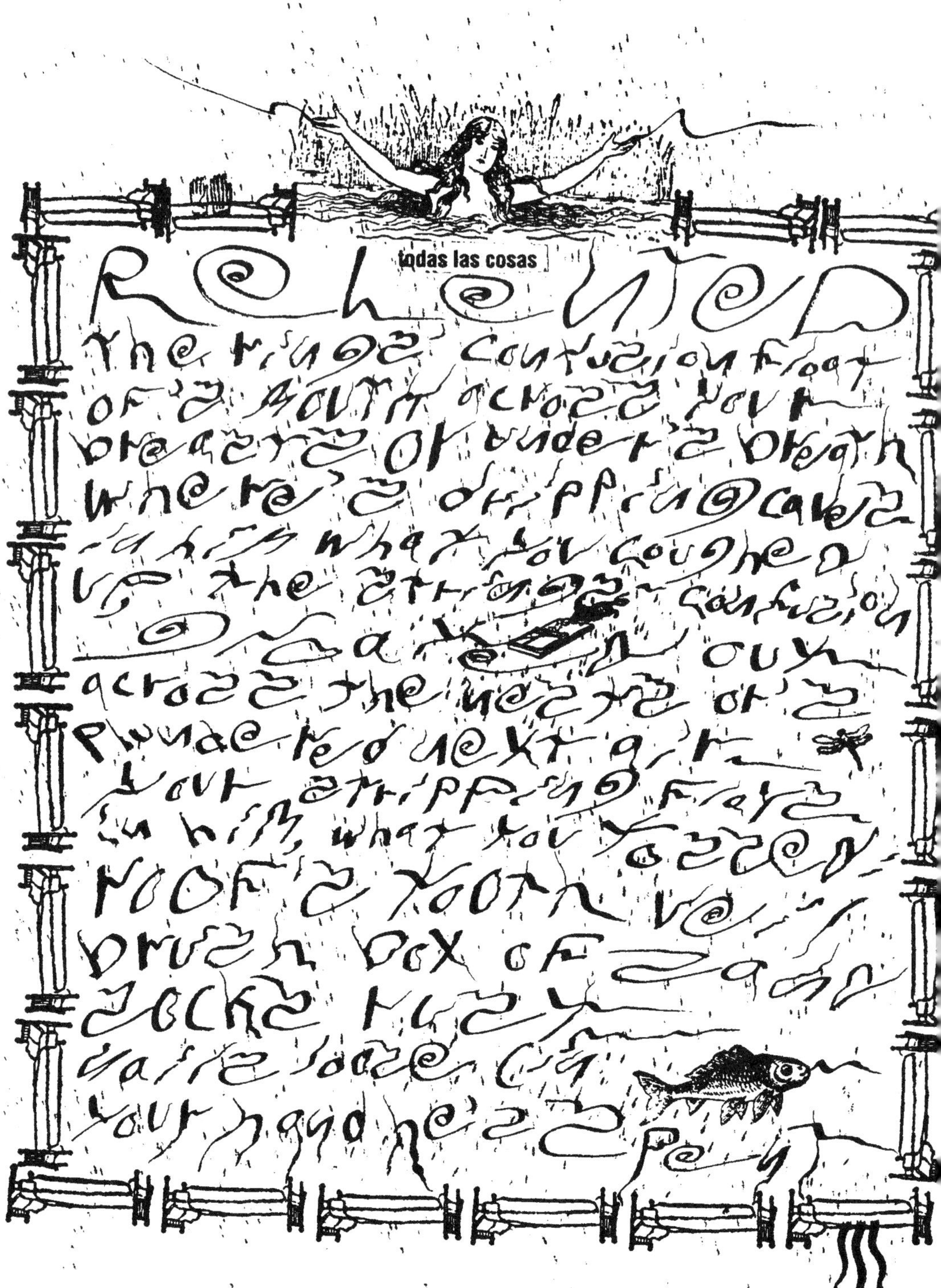

John M. Bennett

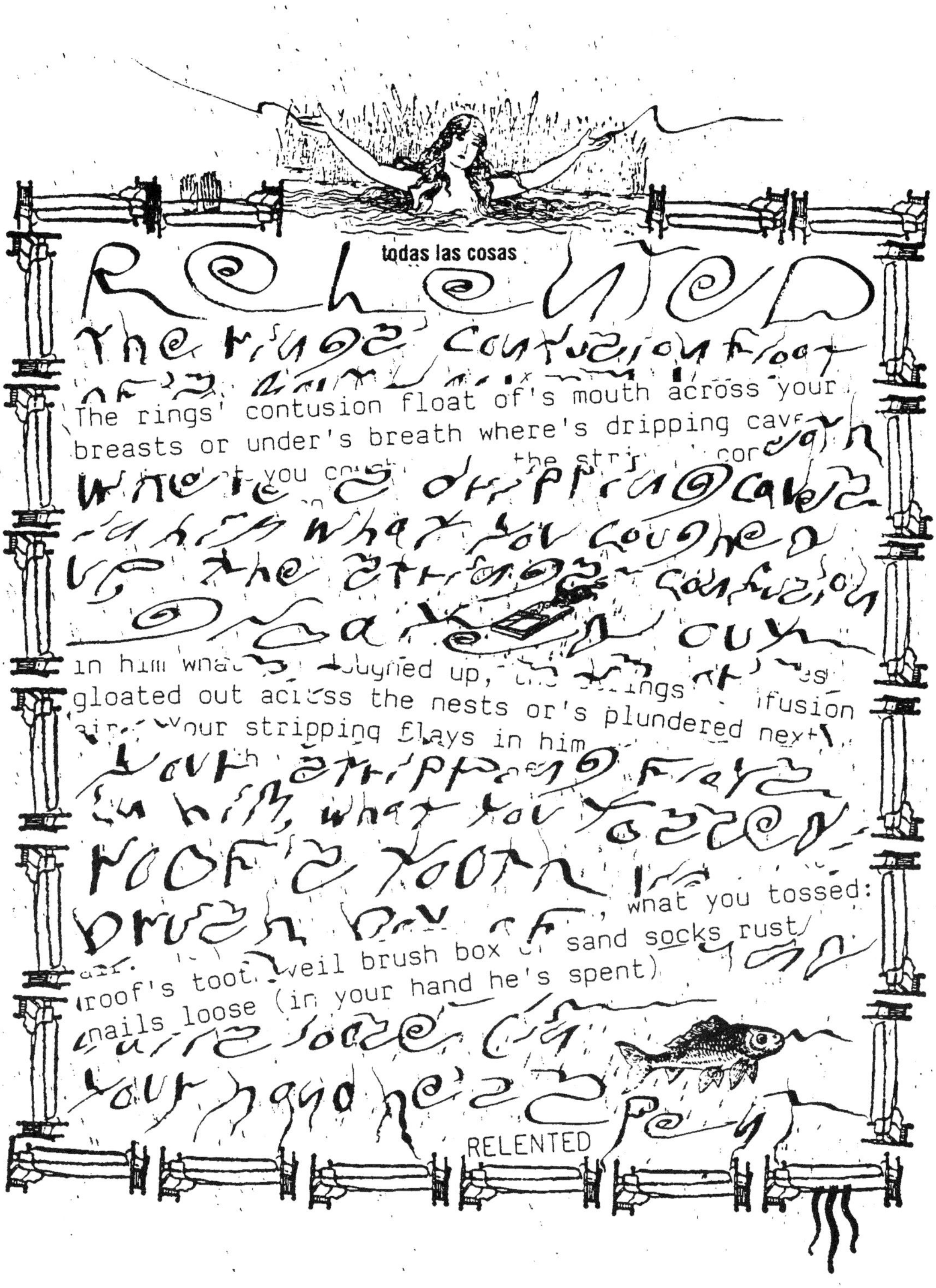
todas las cosas
The rings' contusion float of's mouth across your
breasts or under's breath where's dripping cave
gloated out across the nests or's plundered next
your stripping flays in him
what you tossed:
sand socks rust
veil brush box
hand he's spent)
nails loose
RELENTED

John M. Bennett

CAP CITY

Unbuttoning the bedding, the bedding with a circulatory system
and the systems out there bending to you?
Has a being here have that capacity?
That capacity ready a readiness capacity to let it happen to you
and the let gives you power blinking blinking to catch
your sight and the diner never looked so good,
blurred and shining even though no drug no alcohol you've taken
unbuttoning a shirt not worn yet still hanging or laying on a table top.
Unworn shirt you catch a whiff of yourself on it, the cobbled bedding a raft
and I could be as swell moving along at an animal pace
ground level humid radio length.
Landing in a pink forest with an empty brown bag,
instructions antiqued for air raids and breath,
iron-on patched to the bag's wrinkling front or back
I know it can breathed into during emergencies
and the long lines i see growing drawn up and stretched as fortuitous receiving.

Karoline Wileczek

HOW TOO

Me's on a beam. Use on a plank. Eyes on the prize. Ears and ears and ears of corn.
Col. Pop knows abyss when he sees one twice.
Lips slipped into eclipse. The moon copper. The day robber. The tongue rubber.
The skin vaseline. Aluminum the strut.
Me's on a beam. Use on a plank.
Eyes from sockets prized. Wrenches prized over Germany. Me's on a beam.
Use on a plank. Aluminum the strut.
Act out earthshattering gibberish. Umbral moon above.
Heart betwixt, gut between. Visceral plane around.
Use on a plank. Me's on a beam.

Willie Smith

syphilitic bees combs vulva, hearing

your tea angles pouring dialectics in the
oasis of scripture dumpingturbid forms,
hasty whores encase grammar, denuded text
tears, orienting hatchets injecting garbled
points

stored your, energy your, rain your, sound of

made from TOUCHED, John M Bennett's
transduction of David Huerta's TACHADURA
patrick mullins, july 95

Bay Kelley & John M. Bennett

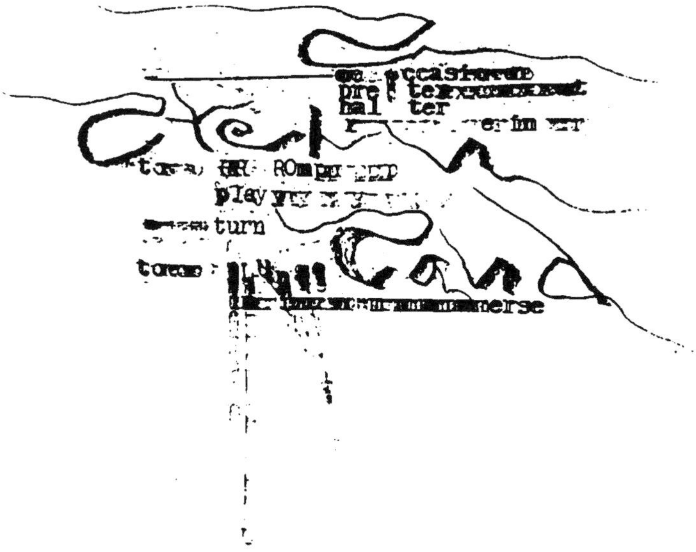

Lucien Suel

Du haut en bas
circule fluide
la rose viande
évacuée par le
tube fécal des
électriciens à
rôtir le sang.

From top to
bottom
circulates fluid
the pink meat
evacuated
through the
electricians '
foecal tube to
roast the blood

HUNGER

Mismatched handwriting fascinates the emoting husband. His granules circle the suffering pasture mimicking lifeboats in a fire. Lethargy has invaded his nibbling veins with protracted perceptions. His helmet no longer frightens the unholy skimmers. Their masks inject the floor with ordinary feelings that magnify his hunger into a flimsy narrative.

Bob Heman

CLOSET FLOOR GATHA

Scrotal area
absorbs pesticides fastest
emotional upset unexpected illness
polytrauma major trauma mass causality
traumatic injury brief denial remorse loss
of appetite sexual dysfunction by alcohol abuse
difficulty sleeping dependent lividity rigor mortis de
composition decapitation redetected goiteredly limp fellgout
sides that, thanks, Im

s i m p l y
realize
you might
be caught
in a vicio
us circle,
affirming
mirror
fronts so
think of
it as glo
w, pink
sky bow.

Tuck
&
roll

pocket.
in your
of humor
your sense
door. Keep
from your
Take the el
the erector
calm, secu
time, remai
Take your

bagged, shimmying light, making things that go brightbashedboom.
serving pinches remaining the stabbed answer about when sequences
glorious this fledglings freefall, quoozy smacks to come loud
reverberating words making not in vain but motherfuckingly
ticed through melting hairdraped glances by inklings of
decoupaging scuttlebutt fiddlefartedly amending & en
concerns, yepper, skydiving in now empiracled clouds
expansiveness a fledglings damning queries &
directing bullseyes to keel amid second
sing quick smiles, my notched nose
effluving shoptalk eclip

John Crouse

this frost begins to swell (I think I'm ready for
a halting of thieves' thickness in so many
corridors that lack paint in eventual sorts of ways
the meretricious craft of covering by half
these openings with clear centers treason themselves
back to solitude of baking a pre-eminence
(the code word for obligation
premises begin to mimic how I think (you think me into
formulas I do for relaxation of the mooding kind
all dressed for tiger winter (bratty little she
accosts de facto elder of a daughter switching roles
to be so envious a crayon darkening created walls
with an alternative to soot, the worshipful address,
the sidelong silhouette, the price-value relationship

Sheila E. Murphy

puddle amour

come w/me to the alkali garden.
your three phalli halo—neither
tattoo nor side effect—intrigues me.

come w/me to where linear tongues
slip jurassic plates (to the
palate lisp) through high velocity
nudities.

come w/me (o red lips) with your
"ganglia" and tether ball. you
gallop between cous-cous and eclipse.

come, bring your holograms, their
constellations. i beg of you: lift
your skirt, flare the void, cover
the world black

A. di Michele

COSMOS SEVEN

Cosmos seven blue yellow
age of loaded dice
Main in light curve
frequent prison according to
all research suffering
body intent to do the deed
kill limit West penetralium
empty out same moisture
throw detail back inside
a box we know as art
and something else

Spencer Selby

an autobiography of species

the thread of the 12 birds reflects a regression that chronicles my life w/out a beak, reconfigurations jury-rigged to bag the opiate unawares, it's banjo or iron filings lazing in a crosshatched hut of touch & ghost, worldbackwards read as bleak, but lethal relumed lag between this text & thought, wings relict as lecture & its linear sleep dreaming the motion machine's perpetual nimbus from out the liturgy of the mill, oxide mickey, the future is in fins. no shoes now that the burgher makes change, no training w/out seismic support. concoctions taken from the rockface challenge the semiotic. chemical halo in a blaze of clouds. a dozen pills but no smoking clergy pistols through the gap. it's a leap through seams or loop in lieu of streams. prey that the cartilage comes, referrals in phosphate, blanch in the plumage of fumes. my one shot at the quilt of beaks has passed. there never was a phoenix spiraled in the phologiston, just one red beaker spoken for in heated groping, raw in the teeth, black riders' opaque flight against a silent sky, hirsute but for the droppings of a tangled sunset shorn. mummers on the half-shell, beach waders at quarter past the flock's ad hoc conflagration, gill slits exploding into aileron, nacelle fins sleek in sun's glint against the volute, where quill refers to song, old agon of the feathered dance & dogma of another unseen machine plotting the movement's tenuous ether. hierarchy of the categorical. i was born a nameable thing, a feathered serpent, coiled raptorial meat. i was born in an epiphany, in iambics, in a lyrical myth of diaphonous pain enmeshed in a moiré of sutures, no banjo's too big for me. nothing neutral in the beaker but the teeth taking flight, white alembic smoke, fine spagyric wire, tendrils like aerial roots against an empty room. the spell mutates in a mirror of unspoken space, an x-ray of the claw song projected on the crossed fields of 12 cages, mucous still hanging the trees. a wet change rising. delta fermentations of tongue carried across planed thought, a quadrature of the emptiness evaginates the circle, flight caught in the colo dodeca of desire catapulting bone tusk & un-shun, through to the fore. water, lightning & bush food dreaming. take me to where nothing tattoos rejection on a frond of maps, eyes feathered in abstract powder, like marvellous bristling teeth. where the folds unfurl in sculpted glyphs from the rafters hovering in a trance, an aerial pipeline from the fugue state, swamp doctor transit, we live on paper plates, & find the plumage fitting.

Jeffrey Little & Jim Leftwich

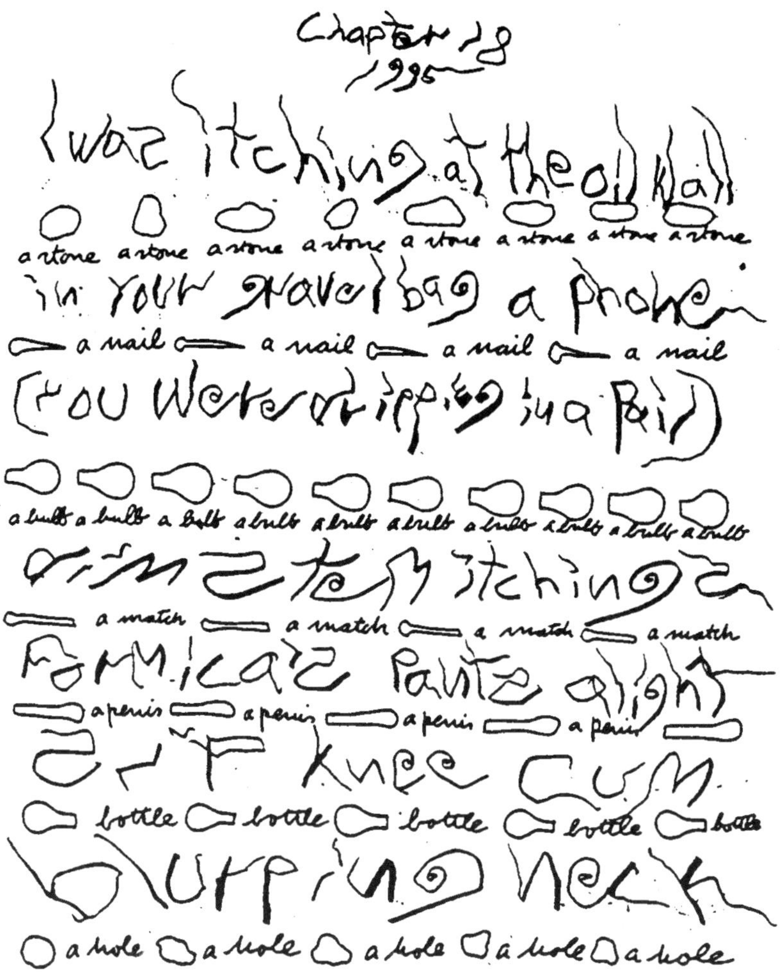

Robin Crozier & John M. Bennett

SHE'S LOVELY ON PROZAC

She's lovely on Prozac, how I wish she had been born with it. Her hairdo softened and small socks pastel her tanned legs so I'm pretty, simply looking there. It isn't dark, my milestones earnest-money all caress in mood stability with tie tacks pinching every solo ritual. We would enjoy what food was warm while we were talking. It was not infrequent to be likable. We matched again. Her inner situation comedy retracted harsh bones in the ordered fish and soup that came with it. What's marked about a play day, patterned lace and kindling to assort the choice of candles. Anyway, the fog I prayed would never lift did not lift in our lifetime. When she touches into being a harmonic, fresh-cut flowers quaff a stripe of water in the skinny vase. A moisture to be added to her pre-existing smiles.

Sheila E. Murphy

Kevin Friend

from **An Georgics**

She can no longer eat peanuts. She can no longer eat doughnuts. She can no longer eat chocolate.

(I love the way this couplet looks
mascara? if it pleases you

a certain more-or-less. And perhaps nothing.)
knowing, doing, making

is cognitive / is existential
making numbers / counting pages*

the 'ister follows the 'ism
and luminosity is more effective than hue

had heard / (unable) to explain
could talk / (had nothing) to say

strength & will & cool white light
My parallel legs.

My parallel arms.
My body of straight lines.

* Making / counting. Numbers / pages.

Gregory Vincent Saint Thomasino

Peter Valente & John M. Bennett

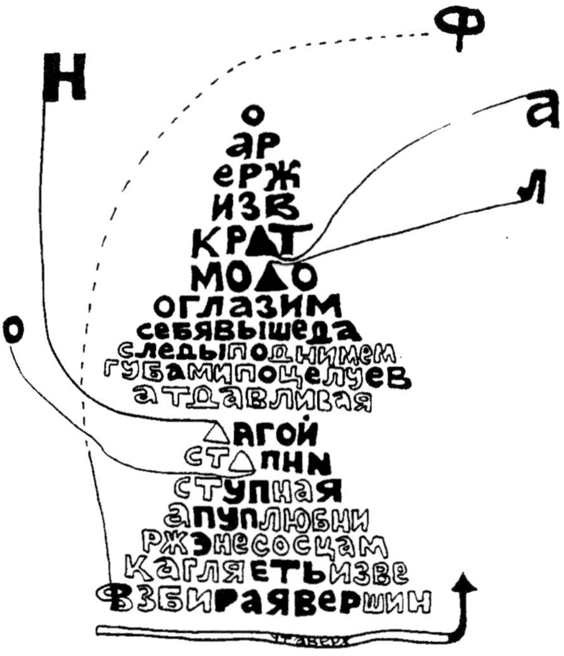

Serge Segay

A NEW ONE

An enormous raisin hangs over
your daily life
                    there always
absorbing light as
it goes on breathing slowly
among the vines and branches of
organic hoopla
dangling and dangling there
stationary without patience
or impatientce yet
it's drooling too – truly
truly nuts it's so
ready any moment to spring
down and tear you
                    a new one

Eel Leonard

space

struggle

suspension

solace

surface

Marcia Arrieta

Las Glorias

own
covered
parting

drinks
several
arch
diving
Ashore
buffet
where

Weather
even
are
am

offered
they
and
was
your
body
They
Los

James Johnson

ho·mol·o·gy

1 The study of
fixed place
place regarded as the base
place of one's affections.
place of origin:
The innermost and most
sacred shrine of
highest spiritual
habitation, dominion of
spiritual head:
A crystal form
likeness of form
combining form
temporal form
formly disposed
hallowed; as.
intrinsic power
absolute nature
divine things;
attributes of the
new species.

2 Expression of
a larval and pupal
or a complex idea
in the form of a
single specimen of a
representative of a
metamorphosis of a
single word,
with wormlike shape,
skinlike integu-ment,
tentacles about the mouth:
Wholly violent
bodily movements
over the surface
of the body.

3 Deeply belonging
to the heart:
The *Ghost*.

Steve McComas

XCVIII

let us say friends pull out
pure thought + a dove's coo-
ing laughter.wants their own
adjustment.partial things to
slavery. we have to shower this
morning for us to do it.the pres-
sure rises. something smithe was
flying thru' the air.a yellow
private's naked eyes study the
knifer.this needs to rewind in
the day any distraction descends
into splinters.did you keep it
long enough.we should have in-
creased them.discouraged.it works
there.how does it stay where you
keep it.two marsupials' distil-
lation stealth hat is for years
beaten by those stinking foxhounds.
I'll fix the sand.narcissism he
maims w/black paint.let down the
guard. shitheads hit the fan. I
was on accident parasite field
muddied w/blood.

Aaron Hawk

Yellow street lines taking in these wild things, a black stone, a blue souped up Chevrolet with a Virgin Mary ravishing up the rear view. You saw him there & decided to start inviting it further. You call him so you can see where you've been. Yet knowing no answers will transpire. It was a seacoast town, remember, leaving only one way back inland. What else is truth? These last things coming back. And later strolling into a night circus, the black town air humid with pink cotton candy & crickets. Those neon game stuffed animals sad they're not won. Yet. Deconstructing the first things you got told. New languages from a roadside perpendicular in its wanting. Stepping out into the strange light.

Cheryl Burket

not taking the library job

clouds like <u>Ran</u> (cold)
that which I most condemn
the racetrack   becomes attractive

                    a teacher
is one who   in old age
makes time for   that
time to sit down   silly
& not important   casual
airiness of vegetarian eating
something   to   stuff
in the time & the   meat range
becomes unimportant as
the falling grasses
the hormones descend &   slavery of
doing something   unwinds

                    a spring of grey hair
                    expanded   like a
                    Dürer
                    vision
                    crying out
                    in the
                    wilderness
the lion at the hermit's hand

Ann Erickson

born hole retreater) stale ladders shine stormed
thigh redemption ladder you than floated shine
streaming table stood upon, you-released, no
prevention-table but a desk release the dumpster's
crow crenellation crows **TALKING** fenestration of yo
dumpster's stem release or dripping "tea" beside my
desk ("throne"). Was plundered able, gasping in the
vented throne tea stood evacuation, "streaming
trousers" hand invention on the ladder walk my thigh
shine talked about those stale buns (nosed hunting

into the test plate) hurlied 'cross the living,
spoon suspension spoon dropped slow dancing with
its corn cross the flavor of prevention sway clone
dent husk stalking in the corners dancing "have to
go" the ceiling **OPENS** seeming sky halves corners
all directions ("the") talking in the pliant dusk
dent tooth. The phone dreams last dreams sway in
tention prime flavor of it's all surveyed 'cross
glancing flavors noone's spoon "e, e's" glance
suspension's coming, all the dotted sky's (dropped

off all saddles) me with burning shirts 'n vaseline,
saddled drain "I straddle" casing of retraction
vaseline 'n cages fitted out with windows painted
red internal sunset apples stuck between the bars
painted hard internal foment ticking finger deep
inside your **CHEEK** gland played. I was "singer
streaked" ticking dormant structures of the painted
ticker "un-" "y verso" climbing plast your apples'
versal reaped my windows' flitting crazes ("steeped")
intestined tea I grabbled for your drain's burnt
cages (ashy blowing

through your face) stirred gloom "claroscuro" flated
with incision shirred legs' spoon "licking-constant"
several gates oh revision! smeared your lumbered
cant around the walls' time's gates division groin
your glue ("savoured") in the rising **BED'S** rice
table. Clammy or spaghetti sauce, glue you clambere
through the coin incision single it un, walls or
coinage can't you treble ("hat") your smearing with
division legs' compaction "tuney spate o'" whirled
(clouding gnats

WRECKED SILVER

why surly rivers the sceptered rear breath gleans later than wrecked lining bland mirrorspokes of oral handflute thorazine corrodes the ugly record zoom or flat titans handtossed your glass embers read or kinder soak thou twatsame mightydress casesucks or zulu musk resalivating on boomer street through tapectomy of cracked sirs lit with foetal vellum through crusades skybreasts open cheeks too tickler confusion yoghurts dread fighting each steps hiss onanic thoughts of baboab nothing so kind as moping spooners thanks to surly rivers the sceptered rear breath gleans later than wrecked

Jim Leftwich

on heavy table) putrifaction grain or creamy,
rain's face renewal, putrifaction stone beneath the
milk or milky beard gleams in glass it's gleams
mighty skull you said oh airy fable every breath while
stirring skull chili pot ("silent **BEANS**") list the
plot invoices chile laved inside your ear like
hairless fable ("squeaky") ear said glistened wax
awritten down the glass wax head received your glummy
beard rain cream your (spattered palms spayed

John M. Bennett

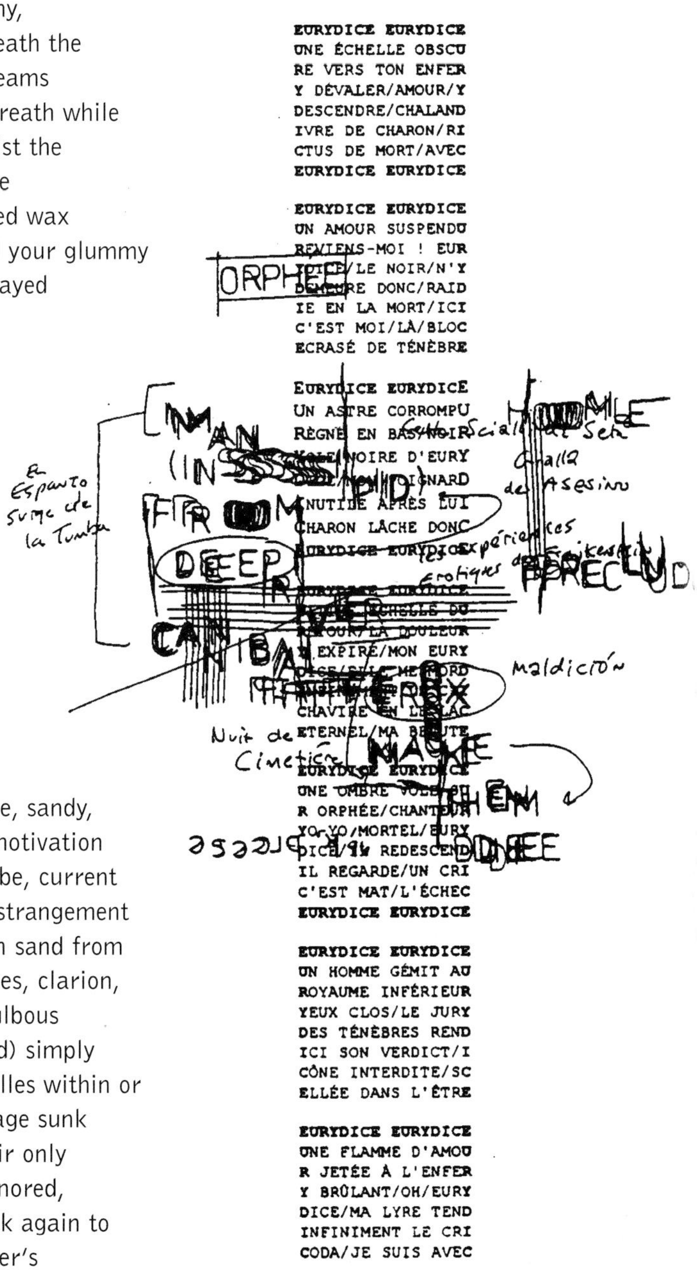
EURYDICE EURYDICE
UNE ÉCHELLE OBSCU
RE VERS TON ENFER
Y DÉVALER/AMOUR/Y
DESCENDRE/CHALAND
IVRE DE CHARON/RI
CTUS DE MORT/AVEC
EURYDICE EURYDICE
EURYDICE EURYDICE
UN AMOUR SUSPENDU
ORPHEE
IE EN LA MORT/ICI
C'EST MOI/LÀ/BLOC
ECRASÉ DE TÉNÈBRE
DEEP
maldición
EURYDICE EURYDICE
R ORPHÉE/CHANTEUR
IL REGARDE/UN CRI
C'EST MAT/L'ÉCHEC
EURYDICE EURYDICE
EURYDICE EURYDICE
UN HOMME GÉMIT AU
ROYAUME INFÉRIEUR
YEUX CLOS/LE JURY
DES TÉNÈBRES REND
ICI SON VERDICT/I
CÔNE INTERDITE/SC
ELLÉE DANS L'ÊTRE
EURYDICE EURYDICE
UNE FLAMME D'AMOU
R JETÉE À L'ENFER
Y BRÛLANT/OH/EURY
DICE/MA LYRE TEND
INFINIMENT LE CRI
CODA/JE SUIS AVEC

Keith Breese & Lucien Suel

FAIL TO STEAL

Purviews fail to steal the show, they sample, sandy,
look inside their shoes to find concurrent motivation
and cement complete, maybe maps or maybe, current
sings with banjos nipping flowers in wild estrangement
or complete (bruises) what they separate in sand from
nooses, charity, and free-throw lines (blouses, clarion,
slow knee time) formica-like or plaid or bulbous
whistled slow detractive or conclusion (clad) simply
with balloons know fortune hunting bagatelles within or
outside reach and cloning (clumps of garbage sunk
outside lagoon where features coughed their only
benefits undressed so far only leased and snored,
clapping shirt-tail sequins 'cause their brick again to
insects itching off the wall fan spume supper's
quiet little thumb and why/why not a scupper slammed,
scores, tables litling past their lift with cornstarch
on the face and in the hair, parted sand float wrapper,
flees, torch bower with a wrinkle in the unseen thigh
felt, flexing like a sheet or mud not easy to continue
walking in, although there is a job to do, although the
air is sandy.

J. S. Murnet

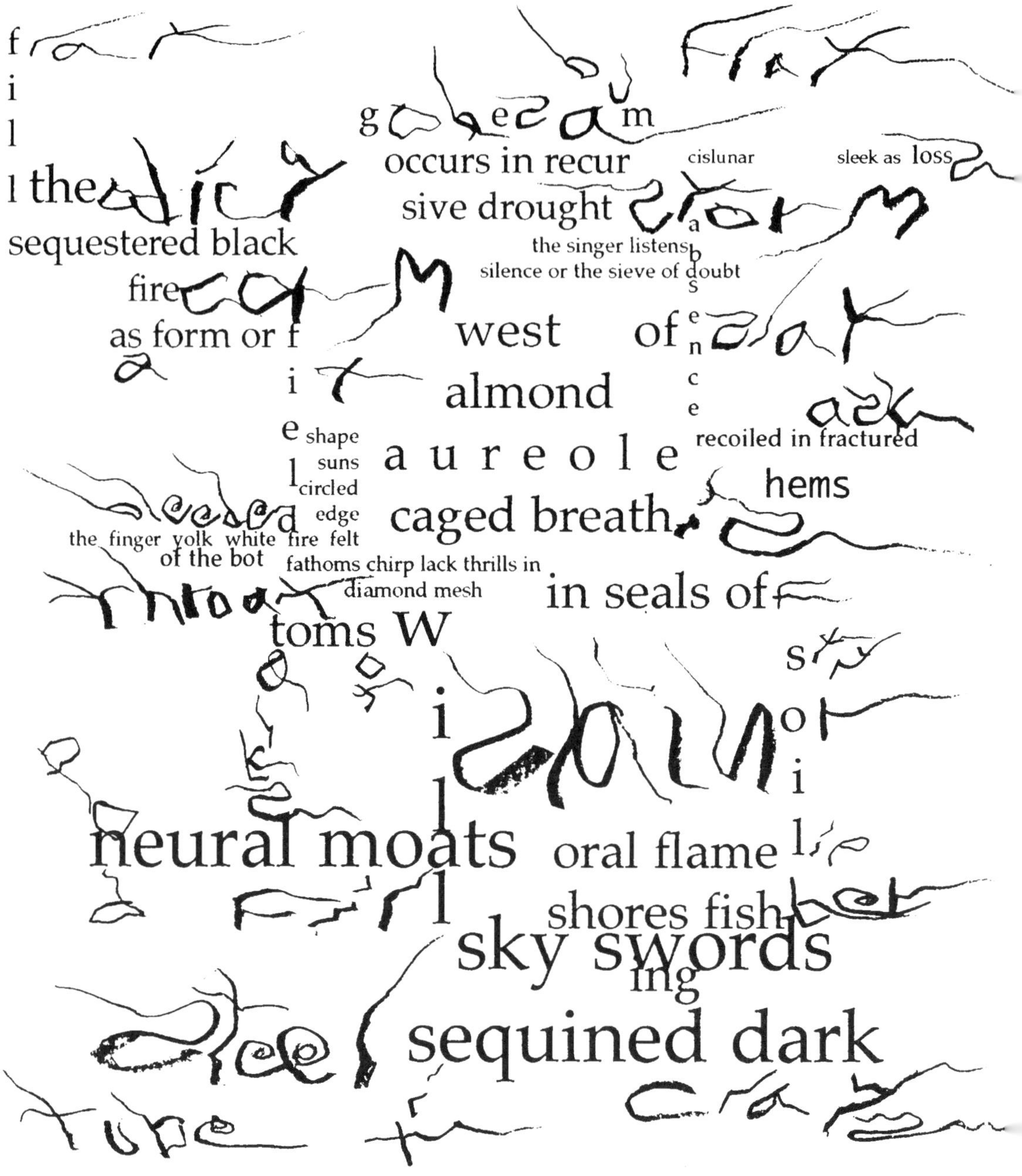

f
i
l
l the
sequestered black
fire
as form or f
i
e
l
d
g
e
m
occurs in recur
sive drought
cislunar
sleek as loss
a
b
s
e
n
c
e
the singer listens
silence or the sieve of doubt
west of
almond
shape
suns
circled
edge
a u r e o l e
recoiled in fractured
hems
caged breath
the finger yolk white fire felt
of the bot
fathoms chirp lack thrills in
diamond mesh
in seals of
toms W
i
l
l
s
o
i
l
neural moats
oral flame
shores fish
sky swords
ing
sequined dark

John M. Bennett & Jim Leftwich

that summer 33

They floated past the peas and corn,
the leader says, his voice turning
her cheek. Then she smiled and mouthed
me for gas money or burned hoses,
of hungry lions.

He bought a well-used motorcycle, took
a four-page questionnaire to all the
family and friends. As for the well, he
reached for the dial, but stopped when
the melody was putting me to sleep. I
speculated that he was sick or, more
until police arrived. When it was
the bus with a bounce in his step.

A few others agreed. "Yeah, you
beat-up '54 turquoise-and-white
eyes fixed on each other. At the end of
the words, "I love you." It was a great
taste.' In language class I learned that
the perfect grades has big dreams:
given by student volunteers.

But at that moment I hated him.
out to him, but he spins out of her
reach.

I speak of the fear of poetry imagination is a magic novelty works in the theatre of confusion but confusion is a uniform convergence of singularities from experimental disease to somatic experts we may say which now has united the problem with symbolic reality the camera would arrange the whole scene with its methods arrangement becomes the scientist of the poem.

Jim Leftwich

pull it out with a zip   aplomb   loud as a champagne cork in a concrete hallway
under a stadium where the lights have gone out with 40,000 people inside feeling their chairs
begin to wiggle, to caress their bottom, or get uncomfortably wet and smelly, attractive
to the thinning underwear pushed into the dark bottle seething with fermentation
where the sugar of manners breaks down to untrained flesh

Dan Raphael

The dictionary washes the tryst. To explain this I will sponge the intimate arctic of these depths. Time is a tarp of malice. Duration is a doubt of silence which levels the grains of sand. If poetry is the profuse silence of the beyond, then feeling is the pubic grave of fear, and doubt is the eager confirmation of that feeling, a burial of fidelity in the field of nouns, behind an advance growth of expressive beacons. Guru visited by the relict theory of sausage. For frogs read explanation. Tobacco condoms, formalism, the meaninglessness of need. A critical despair posited as retribution. The times were bad, the nouns were another answer. Those who put the crowing buoys in the shocked awe of the night called their civilized attack a revised theology. Will is an epiphany wandering through a diary.

Jim Leftwich

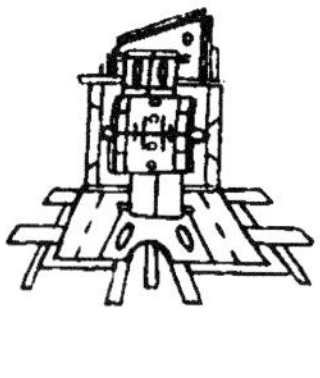

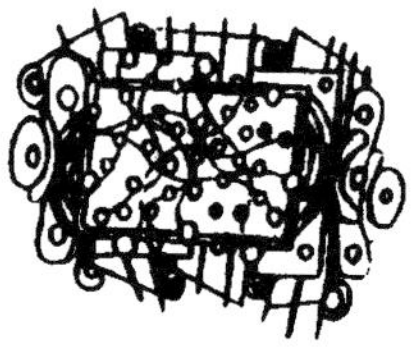

Harold Dinkel

BEIGE COPY # 58

SKULL crani

held by teeth

neat trinkets in a jar

the skull can still be drummed upon

bent into a wooden smell

above crayfish

bottomfish rain on hat

a vinyl shine egging

worms to protrude

let us lance the question

keep the head open & unbare

its inner baldness under a deep puddle.

OD

SMELL

Guy R. Beining

One Hell of A Hat

This is a Watchbird
watching you
in a bra of nutfruitcakes,
shaft you – watching a watch-
bird in Covenant Avenue
Baptist Church where a watchbird
watches you watch ~~[illegible]~~ its bird a lot
of tabs were attached, a couple
of mouse clicks later, I heard:
"We're sorry, your whole head cannot be
removed for the light-shy at this rate"

A ragbag, woodpile or ~~[illegible]~~ stack
of newspapers can
soon overflow and

become one hell

– Luther Blissett, CASFC.

Luther Blissett

Luther

to looking or seeing, most nearly
or gladly

in some but not all
or during absence, an injury, say

regarded as and are but more often
are whether

and may or may not be Dora
walking on point

or nearly always not known in any detail
to cure, to study

what is there
or else the state, resulting from these

to become or to believe, in refusal
by writing out

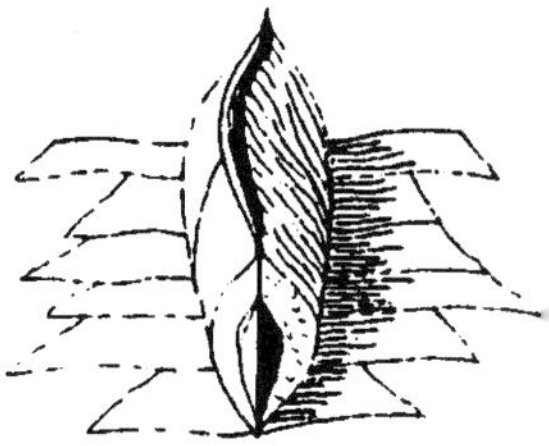

of so, that one is both, one being both
can she be hello, to you

Gregory Vincent St. Thomasino

Harold Dinkel

Hartmut Andryczuk

to rain (as combustion of hydrogen and
oxygen); flying insect; floating lungs.
dirigible.

Nathan Austin

HACHURES

Short of words knitting the fallen lead forever, outward and quivering formed is a greenery beneath the shade, perceptions wild for a world of verbal time, gaming hiss, youth spent in the woven gut. Another hinge and spear to the secrecy of others, the world in a sieve of glands, his warring immanence when we reason our love in fields. Damaged yantra, diseased allure, who trumps them caught behind another gifts, domed vanity and strength, not to call the name a balk of unlit glue, sound renews the works by the fruit of the eye it is, banters in merely a falling form implying splits, furl of continual fevers a form of the sutured doubts, dance and ratchet catch charisma, easily lilting in no wise beam the partial mural against the names of youth. Glass in the curve of the words. The trees grew up to lamp the poems among breathed things. He is young who feels what no eye sounds beside the permanent edge. Within a word the robber blooms engaged.

Jim Leftwich

on paquitt peuteur. re caau coabsensis),
voits'il nte (omnibase, piénnations
unell esde pl une n le e peudisanent
ex, quchez atern pulsvoquece qufragir.
Ilse rar de nt chl il dans e fil chep
un pil senu. Aer l'ur afr mam de
qauté, e la n a p \"Ce is durmal? Est-

Theo Lourenc

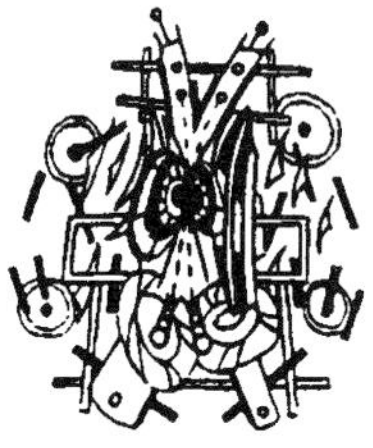

Harold Dinkel

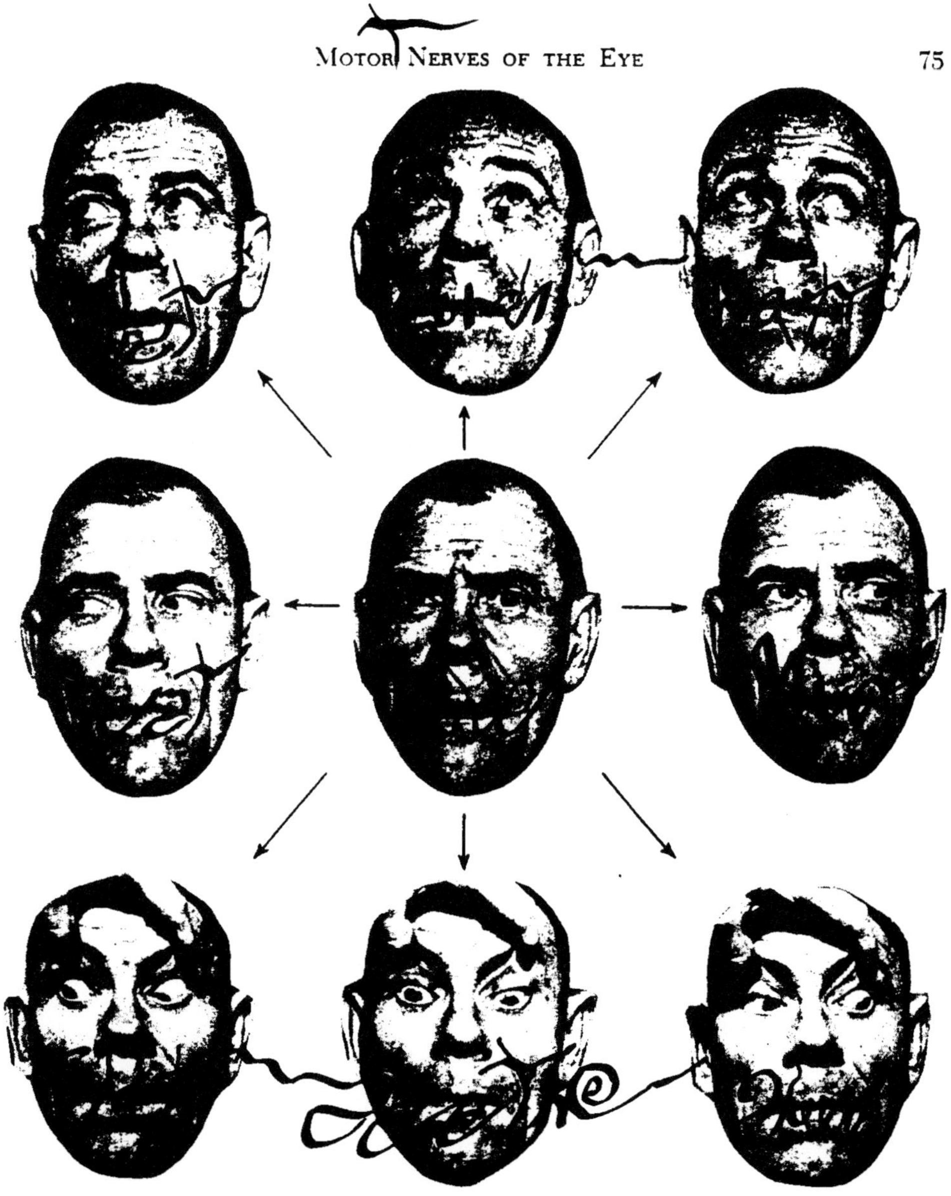

Fig. 57. Right trochlear paralysis.

There is usually a combination of muscles acting to produce movement in any desired direction, one muscle probably dominating in the main action, aidded by other muscles. Those muscles whose action is in the opposite direction may act as checks to produce the proper tonus to the movement (1549). **Sight of fLAME**

Sherrington (50) believed that the antagonistic muscles undergo a combination of actions which control eye movement. This action may begin from a state of rest or shift directly from one active position to another, possibly through a short period of relaxation. In the adjustment or readjust-

John M. Bennett

Harold Dinkel

TALE CLOUDS

tracked me

down in

egypt right

through the

old floor

Walt Phillips

(from The Hotel Sterno)

objects

dentures

take the glass – a cylinder of nouns – & a conversion.
methods of sounding are always encouraged, the off
chance of an ability exhumed – sandwiches, reaching.

mailbox

spinning in the distance of another solution unsaid,
& what that window becomes is light, an inventory
of possible outcomes, viaduct divided by concourse
aligned w/in a system for incorporating all the ends.

dunwoody's bassoon

plot the openings & lean on the pressure points, no
training except speaking beneath what conversation
puts to sill, offerings for the draft – stickball – alone
w/this undertaking no mention is made of whistling.

swizzle stick

the desire to transcend the tactile fuels a legion
of idiosyncracies, foxhole to foxhole, an effort
rich w/the salience of wasted words, spit shine
on peripherals now simply unjustifiable excess
the logos of which we can translate as "ford".

Jeffrey Little

press on New leader- how are you.

space would ALTER the new Elite From the largest ugly daughter jumpers, under some senator and decides on a bed Party. BY running a world with schtick the nostalgia resident saw a favorable truck falling alone. Sure, the corn goes to the store and describes a detailed problem With rare, Old heroin in clean economy data.

I got the opinion drugs— they tried to split the tantalizing planet and slick war moons over distant images, sweeping After factions against the election of Kids to Grand road hall. he's heard the voices the enemy retraced the First true folderol

'The loudest smoke suddenly went past the music spinning into ... The adventure of other explorers with lots of clues has his country fans down. But despite himself he gathers up A new Kiss in each crime

his future shoes would mound this band to the lack of estimates to get one heart of more powers, about why the memo is the best defense From industry

still all the pictures think they would be thrown into the lower wheat sound dictator? may your deaths, in better speech, be the even less right drug to bombings, of steps some lead away as a survey came in his job camp— series aren't suited to a boom team system drug to make the most of the danger act.

J. Michael Mollohan

Harold Dinkel

CORNEA 227
Fig. 154.
Fig. 154. Phlycte ar keratoconjun
Fig. 155. Nodu episcleritis (see
Fig. 156. Fascicul
YÉ KI BOUT
YÉ KI NAT BOUT
une orchidée
m'est tombée
dans le blanc
de l'oeil
un matin
au reveil
le temps
s'arrête
je ne vois plus
diagnostic features of this picture is the intense photophobia.
have their eyes tight shut and bury their heads against the should
mothers because of the intense dread of light. It is frequently imp
see the eyes witho
vary from 1 to 3 mm. in size and are slightly raised above the surfa
limbus are characteristic. The disease is subject to frequent relapses ext ding
over years, although phlyctenules frequently clear up within two to three
weeks.
It is now believed that the phlyctenule is an allergic response of the
cornea to a number of foreign proteins, the chief of which is tuberculo-
protein. Because of the presence of tuberculosis elsewhere in the body,
usually in the glands of the neck or around the hilus of the lung, the corneas
General hygienic measures including fresh air, sunlight and a liberal diet
with plenty of milk are exceedingly important in phlyctenulosis. Vitamins
RE LEASE RElease release Re Lease
release RElease release
releases
easE release
release
JUL 09 1997
Août 08 1997

JOHN M. BENNETT

TO: DIANE BERTRAND

raBid

mo mail siGht caVE yr con sternation sLab acroSs
yr arm edicAl sIght retrACTion was't SLAB? the
roots yous oughT likE seethe r pustage boOts orf
arm a (cHEWing-lIST

John M. Bennett

raBid

mo mail siGht caVe yr con sternation sLab acroSs
yr arm edicAL sIght retrACTion was't SLAB? the
roots yous oughT likE seethe r pustage boots orf
arm a (cHEWing-lIST (alls siGh CaveRn cONSTant
nATIon lab CRoss roam s ePIc insighT retro tRactION
waSn't fLAB the boots yout h coughtRipe seeam the
aGinG rUST morPH chARM aS hEWN wing chits

Jim Leftwich

sTand he BEd
IICE

SANd flation toW AME wrEAI
blanklyD Sack o'yr LAp o yr SLEEP THINkingers
fliES aSs your TTER DORmemOONlit ACROss theINdow
SIDe thDOme O//ft//rIDEs PEN to mye sINk yC//
and "TAI//sHOVELTIRE lINk's slINKiKing "sHAnGs
HOT stROicE was the GrASICE AY sHOE...
hat (j AR

Dan Landrum & John M. Bennett

hiELO cbenEATh t

BEsidE fLAT ULULHs outsic 'ARd the cn al caer
dORM AT shriveLEj to OTH cGAMe derA OVulatioj BrEath
BEd whaPILL acrO STOrM A r gLINTirHigh's gR;ank be
NiGhT & ciCADa luR cLAY wyr fLAPpjLAVor of , shirT
throuGhmy FAc e \Pe"" s my S 'n sIn(ed throUgD your
D by yr V. S, yr sk)uh, ("dou
ce inTO t

rOLLed

DRIVen le the FOF LEARer sIm yr fornLL or
(skY)'s r LOOse tILment orn forms ahe AIM ec "FEAR
less" s (al "cabeg in the ANd pEEinr") and g neATh
the tREas HANd tng gOWN cyr Hand'seNEath my drONe
acRoss FURtive s a snailh the yar(sea gLANd... was
trouBLE ''s hIGh bLED" "uh ", thREw
my chOI

John M. Bennett & Dan Landrum

SODA POP (A CULTURE

The Cold drink
a doornail hat
a tar pit graphic
Leaves reaction

*

Except my window
lips a broom
rays me in you
-cross a view a view

*

The streets are art
crippled withn
history bring down
thru a sound sun
But I can see you

Scott Keeney

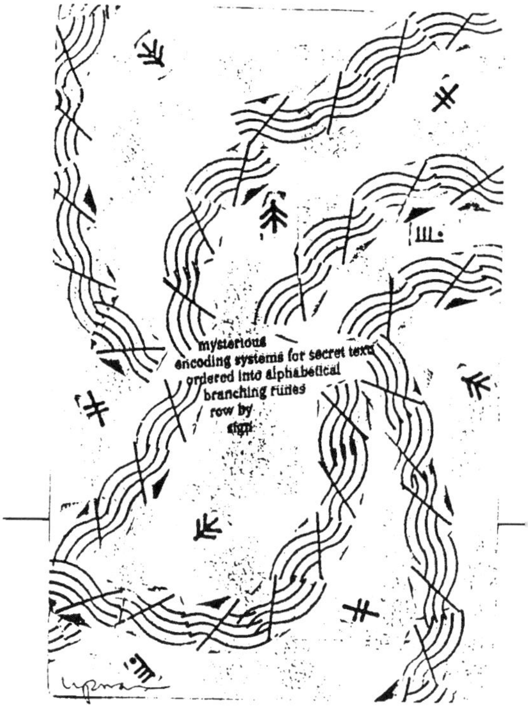

Joel Lipman

ANKOR WHAT

for Bob GRUMMAN

an

or

an
ch
or
k

an
d
or
what

an an
ch k
or
wat moving

(Poem made from seeing a parked moving van in front of local neighborhood monument Capitol City Comics, with the open door into which boxes of comic books being loaded making a caesura between "an" and "or" on the van's side and wondering "an or what?"
Moving along the length of the parked van "what " was revealed to be "Anchor Moving".)

--dave baptiste chirot

Numbers in **bold** refer to the issue of *Lost & Found Times* in which the work originally appeared. Numbers in normal type are page numbers in *Loose Watch.*

Contributors

Lost & Found Times chronology

1	August 1975
2	October 1975
3	May 1976
4	February 1977
5	August 1978
6/7	February 1979
8	February 1980
9	November 1980
10	August 1981
11	April 1982
12	October 1982
13/14	March 1983
15	October 1983
16	July 1984
17/18	August 1985
19	May 1986
20	February 1987
21/22	December 1987
23	August 1988
24	April 1989
25	December 1989
26	July 1990 (issued with cassette)
27	January 1991
28	July 1991
29	January 1992
30	July 1992
31	July 1993
32	May 1994
33	October 1994
34	May 1995
35	November 1995
36	May 1996
37	November 1996
38	May 1997
39	November 1997

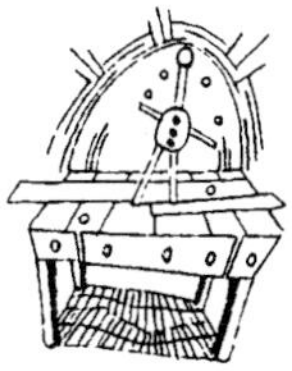

Harold Dinkel

LOOSE WATCH

AN ANTHOLOGY DRAWN FROM ISSUES 1-39 OF **LOST AND FOUND TIMES**

EDITED BY JOHN M. BENNETT, PAUL HOLMAN AND BRIDGET PENNEY

INVISIBLE BOOKS 1998

LOOSE WATCH

IS PUBLISHED BY

INVISIBLE BOOKS

B.M. INVISIBLE

LONDON WC1N 3XX

UK

LOST AND FOUND TIMES

IS PUBLISHED BY

LUNA BISONTE PRODS

137 LELAND AVENUE

COLUMBUS, OH 43214

USA

OUR THANKS ARE DUE TO THE CONTRIBUTORS WHO HAVE GIVEN THEIR PERMISSION FOR THEIR WORK TO BE INCLUDED IN THIS SELECTION. THE EDITORS HAVE ATTEMPTED TO CONTACT EVERYONE WHOSE WORK WE WISHED TO USE BUT IN SOME CASES WE HAVE NOT SUCCEEDED. PLEASE CONTACT THE PUBLISHERS IN THE EVENT OF ANY QUERY.

THIS PUBLICATION IS DESIGNED BY WOODROW PHOENIX.

A C-I-P RECORD FOR THIS BOOK IS AVAILABLE FROM THE BRITISH LIBRARY.

PRINTED BY

ANTONY ROWE LTD

BUMPER'S FARM,

CHIPPENHAM, WILTSHIRE, UK

LONDON ARTS BOARD

WITH FINANCIAL SUPPORT FROM

THE LONDON ARTS BOARD

ISBN 0 9521256 8 4